THE CONSUMER'S GUIDE TO BANKS

Other Books by Gordon L. Weil

The European Convention on Human Rights

A Handbook on the European Economic Community

A Foreign Policy for Europe

The Benelux Nations

Trade Policy in the 70's

The Gold War (with Ian Davidson)

The Long Shot—George McGovern Runs for President

American Trade Policy: A New Round

Election '76

Sears, Roebuck, U.S.A.

THE CONSUMER'S GUIDE TO BANKS

GORDON L. WEIL

A Scarborough Book

STEIN AND DAY/*Publishers*/New York

FIRST SCARBOROUGH BOOKS EDITION, 1977
The Consumer's Guide to Banks was originally
published in hard cover by STEIN AND DAY/*Publishers*,
and has been updated for this edition.

Designed by Ed Kaplin
Printed in the United States of America
Stein and Day/Publishers/Scarborough House,
Briarcliff Manor, N. Y. 10510

Library of Congress Cataloging in Publication Data

Weil, Gordon Lee.
The consumer's guide to banks.

1. Banks and banking—United States. I. Title.
HG2481.W444 332.1'0973 75-12898
ISBN 0-8128-2343-5 (pb)

To

Richard E. Burns

a wise, constant, and generous friend

Contents

Preface to the Second Edition

Banks are by nature secretive institutions. They have resisted publication of data about how they operate and what they charge borrowers and pay savers. While there are signs of change, many banks contacted in connection with this book and other surveys have flatly refused to provide information that could be obtained by an individual customer going to the bank and questioning an officer. The banks simply count on customers not shopping around.

This book is intended as a shopping guide and an exercise in full disclosure. Most of the information provided was current in early 1977, and may now be different in some specifics; it nonetheless gives an indication of the relative charges at many banks and the variety of their services. It is impossible to provide information on every bank in the United States; there are too many of them. But this book is a guide to dealing with your bank, whichever and wherever it may be. It should encourage you to shop around and compare what banks have to offer. Almost anybody should be able to save or make money if he or she shops around.

You can read this book in one of two ways. If you go straight through it, you will have a basic familiarity with the major bank services for individual consumers. (It is not intended for business accounts, although much of the information will be useful for people handling such accounts.) You may consult individual chapters as the need arises, thus using the book as a reference work. Fresh experience will enlarge our understanding of just what banks do, and I would appreciate hearing from you with reports on your own experiences with banks.

This book is not an attack on banks. Many of them are

doing an excellent job of making full disclosure, and some are cited here. The sole bias of this book is that both the bank and the consumer will gain from full and fair competition.

In connection with the preparation of this book, I owe a debt of thanks to Warren Braren of Consumers Union for his encouragement and to Genevieve Gelder for her research assistance. I appreciate the assistance provided by the American Bankers Association. Judith Trumpler and Richard Trumpler, both bankers, gave me valuable comments and suggestions. I also thank Peter Shepherd, my agent, and Sol Stein and Patricia Day.

My debt to Roberta M. Weil, my wife, is more than just pro forma She was the first Commissioner of Business Regulation of the State of Maine and an economist for the Federal Reserve Board. Her advice was invaluable and her influence is felt on every page of this book. Because this book was begun while she was Commissioner of Business Regulation, a job that involved administrative supervision over the Banking Bureau and regular contact with the state's bankers, I have not drawn any of my own data or findings directly from Maine or its banks.

Of course, I alone am responsible for all material in the book.

G.L.W.

Harpswell, Maine
May 1977

1 The Buck Stops Here

There are more of them than post offices.

You'll visit them more often than you'll go to a doctor's office.

They are inspected by the government more than anything but prime beef or buck privates.

But unlike post offices, they are not official institutions.

Unlike doctors' offices, they dispense cash, not care.

And unlike bad beef or raw recruits, they are almost never rejected by the inspectors.

They are banks.

They are perhaps the most pervasive single institution in your life. Their checks create more money than does the United States Treasury. Their loans make it possible for millions to purchase their own homes, send their offspring to college, and provide for their retirement. Even after a person dies, a bank may well manage the wealth left behind.

People have a lot of confidence in banks. An hour after a woman held up a bank in Portland, Maine, the police arrested her as she tried to deposit her ill-gotten gains in another bank.

The bank itself is a go-between—a "financial intermediary"—between savers and borrowers. It collects a fee both for safeguarding your money and for making loans, and pays you for the use of your savings.

What Do Banks Do?

Banks provide services that are some variation on the basic function of acting as an intermediary between savers and borrowers.

The most common service is the checking account. In

almost all cases, the consumer gets a convenient and safe way to handle his or her funds and the bank gets a service fee and the right to lend the money in the checking account and to charge interest on such loans. In only a few instances does the bank pay the depositor interest on the money left in the checking account. The customer is likely to purchase other services from the bank, once he or she has a checking account. For example, the bank must have a safe place to keep its cash, so it installs a vault. Then it rents safe-deposit boxes in that vault to its customers.

If you put your money in some kind of savings account, the bank will pay interest for the use of your funds. Within limits set by law, the savings business is highly competitive because a variety of institutions vie for your dollar.

When you want a loan, chances are good you will go to a bank. Indeed, you may find yourself becoming a borrower almost painlessly by using "loans" created by bank credit cards or by an account that permits you to write checks for more than your balance. From these kinds of loans, you may progress to a consumer loan to finance the purchase of a car and to a mortgage loan, probably the largest debt you will ever incur.

Some people leave to the trust departments of banks the supervision of their funds, both while they are still alive and on behalf of their estates. And you may find yourself the beneficiary of a trust account, often without knowing it, because trust departments handle a great many pension funds.

In providing these services, another thing banks do is make profits. In the decade between 1962 and 1972, their profits rose at an annual rate of 7.2 percent. That growth rate was four and a half times greater than the annual profit increase of manufacturers.

Dog Eat Dog?

In a free-enterprise economy, the push for profits is supposed to heighten competition. Banks like to point out that banking is perhaps the most competitive industry in the United States.

For example, on November 1, 1973, the day when savings banks were first allowed by the government to begin paying as much as 7.5 percent interest, ten large display ads placed by ten large banks on ten successive pages of *The New York Times* attempted to convince depositors of the special merits of each institution. That's what the banks mean by competition, since the law required that the accounts offered by each of them be absolutely identical.

At most midtown Manhattan intersections, three, if not all four, corners are occupied by bank branches begging for business. Many people who run banks believe that convenience—even the convenience of not having to cross the street to get to the bank—is the most important aspect of competition. And that kind of thinking is not limited to big cities. For example, the small and obviously thrifty hamlet of Quakertown, Pennsylvania (population: 2,500), has no fewer than three banks, each within a stone's throw of the others.

A Wealth of Banks

You may find that the competing claims of banks are further confused by the different kinds of institutions. By a tradition that has long since been frozen into law, various kinds of banks have been forced to specialize in certain services.

Take, for example, these three hypothetical institutions: the First National Bank and Trust Company, the First Savings and Loan Association, and the First Mutual Savings Bank.

The First National Bank and Trust Company is a "commercial" bank that may provide all kinds of banking services, including both checking and savings accounts. There are over fourteen thousand commercial banks in the country, not counting their branches. Most claim to be "full-service banks," implying that all of your banking needs can be handled by one-stop shopping.

Because commercial banks have tried to offer the greatest convenience by opening legions of branches, and because of their wide range of services, they are the dominant group of banks. They have a virtual monopoly on checking accounts and specialize in relatively short-term consumer loans. In addition, the words "trust company" in the name of many commercial banks indicates that they have a trust department.

The First Savings and Loan Association and the First Mutual Savings Bank are both "thrift institutions." In many states, these institutions can now offer checking accounts. And they are authorized by law to pay a slightly higher rate of interest on savings deposits than do commercial banks. With the savings placed on deposit, they frequently make mortgage loans. In fact, in some places they are banned from making consumer loans. Thus, the typical loan by a commercial bank is likely to be one for the purchase of a new car. The purpose of the slight advantage given to the thrifts in attracting savings is to ensure adequate financing for needed new housing. There are only six thousand thrifts, far fewer than commercial banks.

Credit unions are still another kind of thrift institution, although they are not banks. The chief distinction between them and other thrifts is that depositors must be members of a specific group, for example, the employees of a single firm or the parishioners of a single church. The members of a credit union get better loan rates than are available from banks, and they may receive dividends after administrative costs have been paid, because credit unions are not operated for profit. In fact, credit unions come the closest to the classical notion of a financial intermediary. Increasingly, they are trying to offer expanded banking services without losing their special character.

Beyond these distinctions, commercial banks and thrifts may be chartered either nationally or by a state. Thus, our hypothetical commercial bank might have been called the First State Bank and Trust Company. As you'll see later, that distinction affects the consumer merely in terms of the regulators who supervise the institution and to whom complaints may be directed. In practical, everyday terms, there's no difference between national and state banks.

The variety of banks and their number, to say nothing of the variety of services they offer, means that the consumer has a variety of choice. By now, it should be obvious that all banks are not alike. It will become evident just how worthwhile it is to shop for banks and banking services just as you would shop for a new car or a television set.

Of course, a new-car dealer is a new-car dealer, and that's pretty simple. By contrast, the names for the different kinds of financial institutions may be confusing. In general, the word "bank" means all of the main financial institutions except credit unions. Among "banks," you can distinguish between "commercial banks" and "thrift institutions." The "thrifts" include "mutual savings banks" and "savings and loan associations."

Who's Who

While banks may be institutions, you have to deal with people. Bank personnel are organized much like the United States Army.

The bank "officers" include the various treasurers, cashiers, and vice-presidents, plus the president and, in some cases, the chairman of the board. Even the directors of the bank themselves take part in high-echelon decision-making, because, under law, they are personally responsible for bank actions.

While younger bank "officers" may be given a branch to operate on their climb up the promotion ladder, members of another group, analogous to "warrant officers," may find themselves limited to promotion within a branch. Their ultimate goal will be to become a branch manager for life.

The "enlisted personnel" of the bank are the tellers and bank-office paper processors. They handle all routine banking operations involving deposits and withdrawals. In larger banks, they may eventually get to handle specialized functions such as issuing letters of credit and transferring funds. Generally, one person is designated chief teller, similar to a top sergeant. In many banks there's also a guard.

An officer will want to see you if you have overdrawn on

your account or have missed a loan payment. You will want to see an officer if you want to open an account or to make a loan. While tellers, and particularly the chief teller, can be most helpful, most often you will want to see an officer (or a "warrant officer") for anything other than the most routine question. The next problem is how to find one.

A Bank Baedeker

Most of the time, the customer's stop at the bank will mean only going to a teller's window to complete a simple transaction. The teller's area is known as the "cage." One window is reserved for the chief teller, and another window—or in larger banks a separate "general cage"—is designated for handling more complex transactions such as foreign-exchange transactions.

In every bank, there is a "platform." What distinguishes the platform from the rest of the bank is that the personnel are sitting down. This area is not usually raised above floor level, although it once was. Now it is separated from the rest of the floor by a rail. There, behind desks, sit what most people think are the officers.

Actually, there may be only one officer on duty, and he's the one farthest away from the entrance to the platform. The absence of office walls gives the aura of openness, but the officer is stationed so that a customer will have to run the gauntlet of underlings—either junior officers or platform assistants—before reaching him.

Everybody gets to the platform at least once—to open an account. The bank would like to see you there again, asking for a loan. But if you have a question or complaint about bank service, you should go to the platform and request to see an officer.

Big Brother Is Watching

Banking is a serious business—deadly serious. Banks hold a large part of each person's assets. If a bank were to fail, those assets would simply vanish.

Government regulators set limits on what banks may do, mostly as a way of making sure they are not grossly mismanaged. In the wake of the Great Depression, several agencies were given authority to ensure that banks are operated responsibly. Deposits were covered by Federal insurance. And the number of bank failures dropped until now and then only a small bank would be forced to liquidate.

While it might appear that the regulators have done a pretty good job, three major Federal agencies stood by in 1974 as the Franklin National Bank sank out of sight. It was the biggest bank failure in American history. Two other large banks—the United States National Bank of San Diego and the Security National Bank on Long Island—also went under in a relatively short period.

While these events have worried depositors, perhaps more than is warranted, they ought to be equally concerned about the amount of policing that the regulators leave to them. Few bank examiners check the bank's arithmetic to ensure that you have been paid the proper amount of interest. And they may not verify the amount of interest you have to pay on credit-card purchases.

In order to look out for your own interests, you need information. Many banks are notably reluctant to make full disclosure, and the regulators are just as likely to side with the bank as with the consumer on matters involving disclosure. In short, while the regulators try to make sure that the bank is managed well enough to prevent it from going bust, they leave it to you to protect yourself.

If Benjamin Franklin was correct in summing up human aspiration as a desire to be "healthy, wealthy, and wise," then banks must take their place in society alongside the doctors and the schools. But if you hope to be wealthy, you'll have to be wise, and by all means, the sooner the better.

2 Your Friendly Neighborhood Bank

Most people simply don't know what they are getting themselves into when they open a checking account. What they are told is merely the tip of the iceberg, and what remains hidden may do them a lot more harm than good.

In part, that's the customer's own fault. Too many people assume that all checking accounts are alike and simply take whatever their friendly neighborhood bank has to offer. Perhaps they will never come to grips with the costs of checking because they will never get into an unusual situation such as overdrawing the account. Other charges, deducted automatically, will be considered a normal price for doing business with a bank.

The convenience of being able to create your own money is obvious—so obvious that the vast majority of adult Americans maintain checking accounts. When you write a check, you "create" money just as surely as the United States Treasury does.

The check makes payment easy. An orgy of check writing can settle the month's bills. And the canceled checks constitute proof of payment and help in record keeping for the tax man. In addition, checks are a lot safer to carry around than cash. An extreme example is the case of the Bronx woman who was held up by two girls. When she told them she had only checks, they insisted she write one out. She urged them to take a check made payable to cash, but one of the girls insisted that the check be made out to her personally. The inept robber was apprehended just as soon as she tried to cash it.

There are more commercial banks than any other kind

of bank, and more than anything else, commercial banks are specialized in the handling of checking accounts. By early 1977, 14,671 commercial banks plus about twice as many of their branches dotted the landscape. And checking accounts make up a large share of the total funds left with banks—some $236.6 billion in 1976. Most of those funds are used for making the loans on which most bank profits are based.

Personal checking accounts are good business. Large banks report that they derive net earnings of 42 cents monthly on each personal checking account—regular or special. Small banks earn an average $1.36 each month on a personal account. In short, it's just as Willie Sutton is supposed to have said when asked why he robbed banks. "That's where the money is," he replied.

As part of their effort to attract new customers, banks offer a surprising variety of checking accounts. Each of them is governed by rules covering service charges and penalty charges, and each customer has to decide on the basis of his or her own use of a checking account which specific plan is most appropriate.

Regular Checking

Traditionally, regular checking accounts were reserved for those people who could afford to leave a sizable balance in their account, in return for which the account was exempted from any service charge. Of great importance to the depositor was the belief that a check written on a regular account would be more readily accepted than a check written on an account where no minimum balance is required. Prestige was attached to having a regular account.

With the wider acceptance and use of checks and greater consumer concern about getting full value for the money spent, this attractiveness of regular-checking prestige has sharply diminished.

In a few places, banks offer completely free checking accounts, thus abolishing at a single stroke any distinction among kinds of accounts. All customers simply have the same kind of account. The American Bankers Association has estimated that 13 percent of the banks provide such accounts, mostly in the Northeast. Banks throughout the country may offer free checking accounts to special groups —students, servicemen, and retirees. Obviously, a completely free checking account is the most desirable for the consumer, except for a very few people who would benefit more from a "package" account. But even in that case, the checking-account portion of the deal has to be the equivalent of cost-free for it to compare favorably with a completely free checking account.

More frequently, regular-checking-account charges are based on either the maintenance of a minimum balance or a combination of minimum balance and the activity in the account—the number of checks written and deposits made. The minimum-balance account requires the customer to maintain a certain amount in the bank, in return for which the account is exempted from service charges. But as the balance falls below the minimum, the charges are gradually increased. At each level down the scale there is a flat service charge, completely unrelated to the number of checks written or deposits made during the month.

There are wide variations among banks in determining the minimum balance for cost-free checking, the steps, and the associated care. Indeed, differences even exist in the calculation of what determines the minimum balance.

The Basic Checking Plan at the Bank of America provides free checking if the monthly balance either averages $600 or does not sink below a minimum of $300. This account thus incorporates both of the most commonly used methods for determining the minimum balance. The average method involves determining balances daily, totaling them, and then dividing by the number of business days in the month. That means a fair amount of math for the bank, but it is a most beneficial account for the customer whose balance is likely to fluctuate considerably. The minimum-balance approach simply requires the bank to determine the lowest balance in the account at any one time during the month. For the consumer who has maintained a consistently high balance but whose account dipped below the minimum on a single day, the service charge is likely to seem unwarranted.

When banks describe regular checking accounts, they usually don't reveal their method for determining the minimum balance. Almost none is as explicit as the Bank of America. For example, when the Chase Manhattan Bank speaks of a $500 minimum-balance account, it means the lowest balance. When the Beatrice State Bank of Beatrice, Nebraska, speaks of a $500 minimum-balance account, it means the average balance for the month.

Of course, a minimum-balance checking account is not actually free. The consumer loses the interest that could be earned on the balance he must leave in the bank. That money is invested by the bank and earns interest, none of which goes to the depositor. If, for example, the $500 minimum were placed in a savings account in the commercial bank for a month, it would pay $2.08. On all regular checking accounts—lumping business and personal accounts together—banks have net earnings of over $8 per account each month. In part, of course, these high earnings are the result of customers usually keeping balances above the required minimum. This is particularly true when the lowest-day-of-the-month minimum balance is used. In such cases, the account is almost always above the required minimum, but the bank, not the customer, gets all the benefit in the form of interest when that "excess" money is loaned out.

The most frequent minimum balance required for cost-free checking is $500, but the figure may go as low as $200. Most often, charges are increased by $1 as each $100 step is passed, down to a floor varying between $300 and $100. The highest flat charge is usually either $3 or $4. These figures are determined by the bank on the basis of the overall behavior of all consumer checking account holders. As a result, any single customer may find that they are either especially economical or unusually expensive for the services rendered.

Charges on "analysis accounts" are based on a specific

examination of just how much the depositor uses the account and how much money the bank has made from lending funds left in the account. These relatively unusual regular checking accounts have been reserved for business customers and individuals with large balances. Because the volume of funds in the account is sufficiently high to provide a portfolio income to the bank far in excess of the cost of maintaining the account, it will pass along some of its profit to the customer by reducing or eliminating service charges.

While it is impractical to offer analysis accounts to all customers, some banks have been able to develop fee schedules based on their actual experience that more closely reflect reality than does the flat rate. The Beatrice State Bank, for example, makes no charges for accounts with a minimum balance of $500. For accounts with a balance of less than $100, it charges 5 cents per check and 75 cents per month. For each additional $100 balance, the 75-cent fee is cut by 10 cents. While the Beatrice Bank is a small institution, the giant Bank of America also provides a rudimentary analysis account. Below the $300 minimum, charges range down from a 50-cent monthly charge and 7 cents per check to an 80-cent charge and 9 cents per check.

Something Special

People who have never had a bank account and who may have limited funds are often reluctant to open a regular checking account because of the requirement of a large noninterest-bearing deposit. As a result, banks developed special checking accounts intended especially for people who both write few checks and do not want to maintain a minimum balance.

Frequently, banks are reluctant to promote special checking accounts because the fees they generate may not cover their maintenance costs. These accounts often have little or no balance that the bank can use to make loans. In addition, these accounts may not lead to use of other services. In fact, many special checking account holders are students and newlyweds and can be expected to use other services later.

Costs and services vary widely. Some banks provide statements only once every two or three months instead of monthly as in regular accounts. While the special account is considered "pay-as-you-go," many banks levy a monthly service charge in addition to a per-check charge. In a small bank, a special account may cost as little as 10 cents a check. By contrast, at the Chase Manhattan Bank, charges reach 15 cents per check, with a 75-cent monthly service charge.

It's worth shopping around for a special checking account because of the wide variation in charges. Within a three-minute walk of each other near Broadway and Fifty-seventh Street in New York, the customer can find the Chemical Bank (75 cents, plus 15 cents a check), the Citibank (15 cents a check, plus a 75 cent maintenance fee that is dropped if ten or more checks are written), and the Amalgamated Bank (no charge but possible disadvantages for frequent check writers, about which more later). For the typical special-checking-account customer who writes eleven checks each month, Amalgamated is likely to be the best bank and will save him or her $28.80 per year as compared with the Chemical Bank.

The "Package" Deal

Increasingly, banks are offering a variety of services, including checking accounts, in return for a fixed monthly fee. All of the other services are less frequently used, so the checking account remains the principal service rendered for the fee.

These arrangements come under many names, with a wide range of charges covering a variety of services. That means that the customer must take paper and pencil to determine if any package deal is advantageous and to compare one with another. Here's how a few of them work.

At the Bank of America, two plans are offered. The

All-in-One Checking Plan is available to those with sufficient credit to qualify for a BankAmericard and Instant Cash, a check-overdraft-loan feature. For a $2 monthly fee, the customer receives personalized checks, a check-guarantee card, the Instant Cash feature, a monthly Timesaver statement with checks arranged in numerical order, a BankAmericard, the right to purchase commission-free travelers checks, and automatic transfer service into, say, a savings account.

Personalized checks would otherwise cost about 30 cents per month. Once a customer purchases these checks, he or she automatically gets the Timesaver statement at no extra charge. All other elements in the package are free to customers who qualify, except for travelers checks, which are probably purchased infrequently anyway. Using twenty checks per month, which the Bank of America says is average, the package would be cheaper than the bank's Basic Checking Plan if the customer did not maintain the $300 minimum balance. If he or she could keep a balance of $300, the interest the consumer would forfeit is $1.25 a month, plus the personalized-check cost of 30 cents, for a total of $1.55, some 45 cents less than the flat package rate.

For $2.50 a month, the Bank of America offers the same package without BankAmericard, the check-guarantee card, and overdraft protection. At first glance, it may appear that the bank is actually offering fewer services for more money, and closer examination indicates that credit services, on which the bank expects to make additional income, have been deleted. Without loan income to offset the costs of the package plan, the bank presumably raised the cost to the point where the plan will pay for itself. Once again, unless the customer is likely to use a lot of travelers checks, he or she may find another account more desirable. Fortunately for the customer, the Bank of America provides prospective account holders with sufficient information about each account to allow this kind of careful choice to be made.

European American has the Bank-Pak. The included services are usually free checks, gift checks (fancy drafts to be used when the depositor makes gifts of money), overdraw-loan privileges (but not free overdrawing rights), travelers checks, certified and cashier's checks, money orders, comprehensive bank statements, credit cards, check-guarantee cards, safe-deposit boxes, and sometimes reduced loan rates.

While all of these features sound impressive, especially for a monthly fee ranging from $2 to $4, many of them are free in any case. Many customers probably won't use more than half of the features provided. Finally, by careful shopping in one or two banks, the customer can probably put together a tailor-made package at lower cost. Of course, for a person who makes heavy use of those services for which charges are usually made, the package deal may be a real advantage.

Strings Attached

Frequently, accounts are promoted as "free," but most of them have some strings attached. Only a few are actually free of fees and do not require a minimum balance. Often, "free" checking accounts are package arrangements, with the bank implying that the service charge covers all other services. Closer examination will almost always reveal that the service charge is essentially related to checks and not to less frequently used services. In other instances, "free" checking accounts involve a minimum balance, perhaps somewhat lower than those associated with regular checking accounts. If, for example, an account were "free" except for a minimum-balance requirement of $200, the actual cost would still be far less than the service charge for a regular or special checking account. The interest that you would lose on the $200 would be no more than $10.94 a year. Service charges would surely be more.

NOW Is the Time

With the exception of the relatively unusual free checking account, you have to pay for the privilege of having a checking account, even though the bank may be earning interest on the funds you leave on deposit. Businesses and large depositors who have a lot more clout than the average customer were able to induce banks to create analysis accounts, which might at least eliminate service charges. Then, some businesses insisted on unused funds in checking accounts being automatically shifted into interest-bearing accounts. That meant that interest payments on short-term deposits could actually exceed service charges.

The individual was pretty much left out of such arrangements unless the account involved was quite large. Then came the NOW account.

The Consumer Savings Bank of Worcester, Massachusetts, recognizing that a statement savings account was quite similar to a checking account, sought approval to allow account holders to withdraw funds from their accounts, not by presenting a withdrawal slip to the bank, but by giving the slip to a third party who could present it at the bank. Previously, when the account holder had been required to make all withdrawals directly from the bank, the withdrawal order was considered "nonnegotiable," or nontransferable. But by passing what in effect is a communication between the account holder and the bank through a third party, a "negotiable" order of withdrawal was created. It took a favorable decision by the Massachusetts Supreme Judicial Court before the NOW account became legal.

NOW accounts—in effect, checking accounts on which interest is paid on the unused balance—were soon offered by other thrift institutions and then commercial banks in both the Bay State and neighboring New Hampshire. But soon after the thrifts began popularizing the NOW accounts, commercial banks brought pressure in Congress, which blocked their extension into states outside New England. The legislative rationale was that NOW accounts were experimental and their impact on commercial banks had to be tested.

In fact, NOW accounts are immensely successful because they come closer to fairly repaying the depositor than any other kind of account. But they obviously reduce bank profits on each individual account. If they failed to attract new funds into the bank, the amount of funds available for longer-term loans would be reduced.

At first, Massachusetts and New Hampshire banks levied service charges of 10 and 15 cents per check, much like a special checking account. Since the accounts obviously involve expense for the banks, such charges seemed fair as long as interest was paid to the depositor. Even if a very small balance is maintained, the NOW account is preferable to a special checking account because the interest will reduce the fee. The Provident Institute for Savings, a large Boston mutual savings bank that quicky followed the lead of Consumers, levies no charges if the minimum amount in the account exceeds $500. But the depositor receives interest on that minimum account. In short, with or without service charges, the NOW account is better for the consumer than any checking account.

The commercial bank response was to create NOW accounts for their savings account customers. At the same time, they waged an ad campaign to discourage use of these NOW accounts on the ground that people would be tempted to tap their savings. They argued that savings should be kept inviolate and inviolable.

The greatest obstacle to attracting new customers has been the service charge, and as a result, more than half of all banks offering NOW accounts have dropped them.

Due to the congressional action resulting from commercial bank pressures, the NOW-account banks are not to solicit accounts from out-of-staters, and most have discouraged such accounts for fear of stimulating even more restrictive legislation. Even without advertising, they received requests to open such accounts and have done so, although in some cases they have imposed high minimum balances.

Banks in other states were eager to get a piece of the

action. Some savings institutions are authorized to open checking accounts, but they cannot pay interest on unused balances. According to Consumers Union, all savings banks can also provide checking accounts. The Kansas Credit Union League has actually purchased a bank and has offered free checking to members. Credit unions now issue "share drafts," the equivalent of checks. Commerical banks have protested this action which helps make the credit unions into full-service financial institutions. But, by March 1977, more than 700 credit unions were offering share drafts. The payments under this service amounted to about $170 million a year. Although this is a small portion of the total amount of money transferred by checking, the use of share accounts is increasing at a rapid rate.

In 1974, an effort was made by New York banks to get around the law. They offered an arrangement allowing for either automatic transfer of funds from a savings to a checking account or transfer made in response to a telephone request. The New York Banking Superintendent cracked down, forcefully reminding savings institutions that they could not make transfers, except in writing. New York's "payment orders" fizzled. Even so, the Brooklyn Savings Bank ran a series of misleading ads designed to give the impression that it offered a single account that paid interest and provided payment orders. Actually, the small type in the ad revealed that it was two accounts. No interest was offered on the payment account. It finally took legislative action to allow New York savings banks to offer checking accounts.

Of course, a do-it-yourself NOW account is possible if funds are left in a day-of-deposit–day-of-withdrawal account and withdrawn, say, only once a month. As many checks as possible should be written at the same time as the transfer has been made or perhaps a day or two in advance. That means interest will be paid up to the last minute, when the funds are needed to cover the checks. Such a system requires either a trip to the bank or making a mail withdrawal regularly.

For those who need few checks and do not mind an occasional trip to a thrift institution (or making a mail withdrawal), the use of savings bank or savings and loan association checks may take the place of a checking account. On day-of-deposit–day-of-withdrawal accounts, interest is paid until the check is written. The thrift's check is made payable to any third party at your request. This amounts to an interest-bearing checking account.

The Citizens Bank and Trust Company of Chicago has worked out still another scheme. The United Security Account, marketed with a lot of razzle-dazzle that is sometimes misleading, is actually two accounts. You open a savings account and automatically receive what amounts to a line of credit of the same amount as your balance. You may write checks up to the full amount of your savings account balance. However, no interest is paid on that part of the savings account balance equal to the value of outstanding checks. If you do not deposit money to cover the outstanding checks by the fifteenth of the month following the one in which they were written, you begin to pay 6 percent annual interest on the amount of the checks for which a new deposit has not been made. There are no service charges.

The Chicago bank says it has 190,000 USA holders in all fifty states and abroad. Even though the bank provides an identification card, it is likely that some of these people would encounter difficulties if they tried to pay for the week's groceries with a Citizens Bank check, which does not even look like an ordinary check. The account is perhaps best for a person who can have a deposit made regularly to the account and who writes relatively few checks. Indeed, the bank itself uses the testimonial of a foreign correspondent in Cairo to sell the virtues of the account.

But the United Security Account may be useful for those people who can manage with two accounts—one for local needs and the USA for mail payments and for those local merchants who will accept it. The problem with local acceptance is not only that merchants question the validity of the check; it may take several days longer for funds in a Chicago bank to be credited to their account.

Citizens pays the highest day-of-deposit–day-of-withdrawal rate allowed to commercial banks. In 1977 that was 5 percent. But remember, if you don't make a deposit equal to the dollar amount of the checks you've written, you must either tell the bank to withdraw the necessary amount from your savings, or "borrow" the money to cover the checks. This "loan" carries a monthly interest rate of ½ of 1 percent, a 6 percent annual rate. You pay interest only on the outstanding loan balance, not on any interest that may still be due. And because your account balance continues to earn interest at almost the same interest rate as you pay on your outstanding loan, the net cost of the account is likely to be less than the cost of an ordinary checking account.

The USA account has not been copied by other banks, although it now has been offered for several years. In part, managing the account is more costly than an ordinary account. Of course, Citizens knows that its account holders will not write a great many checks on their accounts. Thus it profits from a higher rate of return on the investment of deposits than is ordinarily possible for a commercial bank that cannot expect deposits to remain in the account for so long a period. In addition, most commercial banks want to avoid for as long as possible paying interest on checking accounts or even seeming to do so.

New York's European-American Bank has a variation on the USA account, but the benefit to the account holder is far more doubtful. Under its plan, you open both a checking and a savings account with a minimum balance of $500. European-American charges a flat $1 monthly fee for the checking account. This plan must be compared with the two other European-American checking accounts. The activity plan costs 15 cents per check plus a 75-cents-a-month maintenance charge. Unlimited checking is free if the checking account balance exceeds $500, while $2 fees are charged as the balance declines below that level. If a customer maintaining a $500 balance writes twenty checks a month, the net position for a customer using each European-American account would be (using 5.5 percent interest rate):

Type of Account	*Savings/ Checking*	*Activity*	*Unlimited*
Service charge	−$1.00	−$3.75	0
Interest	+$2.29	+$2.29 *	-$2.29 *
Net (gain + or cost -)	+$1.29	−$1.46	−$2.29

* If $500 placed in savings account.

Obviously, the savings/checking account is cheapest. But the monthly difference of $2.75 between it and the activity plan must be weighed against the inconvenience in obtaining funds from the savings account when needed. For that very reason, it's impossible to work the savings and checking accounts in tandem in any way similar to the USA account.

Out of this welter of ways to create an interest-paying checking account, some order is now beginning to emerge. In April 1975, the Federal Reserve Board in Washington announced that it would permit banks to allow their depositors to withdraw funds from their savings accounts by phone. For the preceding thirty-nine years such withdrawals had been banned.

Interest-paying checking accounts should soon be available throughout the United States. The "experiment" with NOW accounts has to be deemed a success, so there's no reason not to extend it to all states. In fact, Federal Reserve Board Chairman Arthur Burns has proposed such a move, but has suggested that the interest rates of 5 percent originally paid on such accounts may have to be reduced because it costs the banks more to handle NOW accounts than traditional checking accounts. With virtually all banks—commercial and thrifts—able to offer NOW accounts, consumers would be the biggest winners.

Banking-by-phone

Perhaps it was inevitable that the telephone would replace the bank check for a great many transactions. The 1975 Federal Reserve ruling on making withdrawals by phone certainly speeded up the process. Since then, more and more banks have begun offering banking-by-phone services.

You must sign up in advance for this service and be assigned a security code to be given to the banking operator in addition to your account number. Then, you may call during designated hours and request that funds be transferred to a third party, most often a company which has billed you. Using computers, the bank debits your account and sends a mesage through the check-clearing network to inform the company's bank that its account should be credited with that amount.

Obviously, banking-by-phone works well with a NOW account, because your money keeps earning interest until the moment you call. Where NOW accounts are not yet authorized, thrifts can take phone orders to transfer funds from a savings to a checking account and then to make the payment desired. Typical charges for banking-by-phone are 15 cents per transaction with a minimum balance of $100 or 10 cents with a $300 minimum. Such charges are likely to be lower than the combined cost of postage, checks, envelopes, and your effort in paying by mail. In addition, some services may be called 24 hours a day.

You may find some drawbacks to banking-by-phone. You receive a statement monthly indicating all transactions, although payments will have been deducted from your accounts as they were made. That means a special effort on your part to deduct each payment from your balance whenever you call it to the bank. In addition, you do not receive a cancelled check as a receipt for payment. The statement will serve this purpose adequately, because it indicates the amount paid, to whom and when, but it may not be as handy as having the actual checks available as proof of payment. Finally, only a few out-of-state companies are likely to be covered by your bank's phone accounts. Some banks will try to make arrangements with a distant company if you make regular payments to it, but, in some cases, banking-by-phone will not be much help.

In the last analysis, convenience is the most attractive feature of any checking account and banking-by-phone certainly adds to that. As a result, a steadily growing number of banks can be expected to offer the service.

Self-expression on the Cheap

It's a good picture. It lifts the spirit. The crystal-blue surf pounds the rocks at the base of a towering cliff. Bright sun and fluffy clouds promise a splendid day. Matisse? Gauguin? Grandma Moses? No. Behold the lowly bank check in all its glory.

Banks all over the country now sell so-called scenic checks. In addition to providing a little something for the soul, they also provide the convenience of printing the name and address of the account holder on the checks, a convenience when cashing them, plus prenumbered checks. Prenumbering allows the bank to list the checks in numerical order on the statement, which helps some people get through the onerous task of reconciliation.

Customers so badly want to express themselves when they write checks, according to the ABA, that they prefer to pay a charge to get a scenic check rather than no charge at all for a plain, old-fashioned bank check.

Perhaps customers actually are willing to pay more for a pretty picture, but other explanations are possible. When a customer opens a checking account in most banks, he or she will automatically be offered the opportunity to purchase scenic or at least personalized checks. Mention is often made only in passing about regular bank checks. Alternatively, the customer may actually be given these special checks as the first supply from the bank. The reorder form urges purchase of the same kind of check or another scenic type. It does not mention cost. Instructions for ordering regular bank checks are usually in smaller print and more difficult to find. Sometimes the bank simply expects you not to find the box to check for cost-free checks. One man who placed his first reorder at New York's Chemical Bank and asked for standard checks, nevertheless received personalized checks. Only after he went to the bank and complained was he refunded the check fee that had automatically been deducted from his account.

Even if the customer wants scenic checks, he or she will have a hard time figuring out the cost. The sample books do not contain prices, and frequently the platform personnel are completely uninformed. As a result, you may have to wait until you have actually begun to use the scenic checks and have received your first statement before the cost of the scenic checks is stated. In a survey of banks in the New York area, the cost of an order of scenic checks (usually two hundred) ranged from nothing to $5.10. Unlike the period when banks charged for each blank check in a special checking account, if you spoil a scenic check, you cannot go to the bank and get a free replacement.

Only a few banks do not issue cost-free stock checks. If the way a customer wants to manifest his or her personality is not pictorially but pecuniarily, then the free check is the best way to a better life. Unless, of course, you'd like the ultimate—the check with your own picture on it.

Let Me Make One Thing Perfectly Clear

Obviously, the check is at the heart of a great number of the financial transactions in an average person's life. By the time the customer gets his or her canceled check back with the monthly statement, this bit of paper may have made a long and sometimes tortuous journey, much of it recorded on the back of the check. The whole process is called "clearing."

Ordinarily, check clearing should be a matter of small importance to the customer, but in fact, it may be a matter of money. Most banks tell you in the fine print on the signature card when you open your account that you cannot draw checks against other checks you have deposited until they have cleared. That means that your bank wants to make sure that the person who wrote you a check has sufficient money in his account to make good on it before the bank lets you use that money. Fair enough.

The trouble is that the individual depositor has no idea just how long it takes a check to clear, and he or she may draw on uncleared funds. If so, the depositor's own check will bounce. In fact, the most frequent cause for a check's being returned for insufficient funds is drawing on deposits not yet credited to the account.

In most cases, depositors do not run into this problem, of course, because their own checks are in the process of being collected a few days after their deposits enter the same process. As a result, the individual is in effect gambling that his or her own check will not reach the bank until after the check deposited clears.

The best bet is for the depositor to ask just how long the banks allow for checks to clear. The survey of New York area banks by the New York Consumer Assembly showed that banks allowed from one to eight days for in-state checks to clear and from three to twenty days for out-of-state checks to clear. There is virtually no justification for such a variation because all banks use the same facilities for clearing checks. In New York, in-state checks—and certainly those within New York City itself—can be cleared within twenty-four hours by a continuous computerized process. In any case, banks that say they require as much as eight days are obviously giving themselves a wide margin of security.

In fact, they are doing more than that. They are making money. When a prospective customer asked at the Amalgamated Bank how they could offer completely free checking, he was first told that statements were issued less frequently than normal. When he pressed for a better explanation, he was told that his initial deposit would not be credited to his account for eight days.

What happens is that the bank is informed that the

check has cleared within twenty-four to forty-eight hours on local checks. But it delays depositing the money to your account for another few days. During that period, the bank can use your money for a variety of purposes that will earn it interest. This procedure is actually not one of the traditionally legitimate earnings functions of a checking account.

At Chemical Bank, a customer was told that although the bank had been credited with funds from a local check within forty-eight hours, that money would not be deposited to his account for an additional forty-eight hours. The bank argued that it would wait to see if the check bounced. It preferred to withhold the customer's money while waiting rather than run the risk of having to withdraw money from his account later to cover the bad check.

While few banks will state just what proportion of their customers write bad checks, Chase Manhattan says that 2 percent of its personal accounts are overdrawn at any given time. It's questionable whether or not it's fair for banks to refrain from depositing 100 percent of all funds that have cleared on the grounds that 2 percent might have to be withdrawn again.

Checking account customers should understand that the delay in crediting deposits to their account can cause a real inconvenience. As in the case of Amalgamated, it's worth finding out. Of course, for some customers the problem of delay will never be of any real importance. If it is a potential problem because, for example, you need to withdraw money from an out-of-state paycheck, you should ask a bank officer for special authorization to draw on uncollected funds—uncleared checks. Particularly if you maintain a reasonable balance and are a good customer, the bank should be willing to grant you this convenience at absolutely no cost.

A Simple Declarative Statement

Next only to the fun of writing checks is the joy of receiving a bank statement and trying to reconcile what the bank says you have with what your checkbook says you have. Many people don't even try, although the process is not as complicated as it seems. The bank is not infallible and the only real check on the accuracy of its bookkeeping is the customer's reconciliation of his or her checkbook with the statement. Even for the most lazy, the statement is a useful way of starting afresh, but that means you have to accept the bank's version of your balance.

Either way, it's useful to receive the statement as often as possible—in most cases, monthly. Some banks that offer low-cost special checking accounts or free accounts provide statements only once every three months. These will be satisfactory only to the person who makes light use of the account. Unless you're a very good keeper of the book, you're bound to make some error in a three-month period. So it's worth deciding whether the extra cost of the service charges for monthly statements isn't warranted.

Banks have been introducing consolidated or comprehensive statements that provide information not only on the checking account, but also on outstanding loans, savings accounts, and credit-card accounts. The benefit for the customer is that he or she can see at once the status of all accounts and loans. Yet many customers do not want others, even at the bank, to see the status of all accounts and loans. As a result, banks have had to offer customers the right to delete any information they wish. That's important to know if your bank uses a comprehensive statement as a matter of standard practice.

The bank probably benefits more from the comprehensive statement than does the customer, because the statement itself is a powerful selling tool for a variety of services. Unless you have a savings account where you normally receive a statement instead of having entries put in a passbook, much of the information will be of only limited use. You will still need to use your savings passbook, and you will still receive a separate credit-card bill. Of course, when the customer sees just where he stands, he may notice that he's paying the bank more for a checking account than the bank is paying him interest on the savings account.

While the consolidated statement doesn't make money

for the bank or cost the customer anything, it is primarily a marketing tool. Before a customer is attracted to a banking service by the existence of this statement, he or she should probably weigh the utility of what's being offered.

A Little Something on Account

Banks like deposits and provide special services in order to make sure they attract all they can. Only in certain activity accounts do the banks charge for deposits. Some banks will even pay your postage on deposits by mail.

Preauthorized deposits can often be arranged with disbursing agents of companies and with employers for the automatic deposit of dividends or salary checks. The bank likes this procedure because it has funds on hand it is certain will clear, perhaps a day or two earlier than otherwise would have been the case. The customer is discouraged from spending more of the funds prior to deposit. At the same time, the customer can probably draw on the funds earlier and is saved the inconvenience of making a deposit. In case of either a dividend or a payroll deposit, the customer should receive notification at the time the deposit is made from either the depositor or the bank, or both.

Frequently, banks will offer to make automatic transfers out of the checking account into savings or loan accounts. This saves the customer the need to write checks and removes the problem of remembering the required loan payment. Usually, this automatic transfer feature is free. But the customer should ask an officer, because some banks charge the same amount as if a check had been written to cover the cost of the transfer.

Cash and Carry

Sometimes the customer will want to make sure that his check will be as acceptable as cash. In short, he wants the check to be accepted immediately, not subject to collection.

A customer can obtain a certified check simply by using one of his or her own checks. It must be taken to a teller's window. The teller checks the amount of money in the account and immediately withdraws an amount equal to the check. That means that funds are immediately deducted from the account, not when the check clears. The bank will identify a certified check by strange strips and punched holes, so that when it is processed, funds are not inadvertently deducted a second time. This service should be absolutely free because it amounts to nothing more than writing a check and preclearing it. Yet the New York area bank survey showed that most banks make a service charge. Often, on request, they will forgo the charge.

A cashier's check serves the same purpose. It is a check signed by the bank itself and thus widely acceptable if the bank is well known. In order to obtain a cashier's check, the customer must present cash. Of course, funds can be drawn out of a checking account, so the customer will not have the cost of a check. And there is almost always a service charge for a cashier's check. In addition, not all banks make them available to the public. Occasionally, banks issue so-called gift checks, which are nothing more than cashier's checks in a fancy wrapping. It's actually more economical for a customer who is confident that his or her check won't bounce simply to write a regular check and send it with an appropriate greeting card.

In most cases, a savings bank or savings and loan will issue a cashier's check at no charge to cover a withdrawal from the account.

Most banks also issue money orders, which are virtually the same thing as cashier's checks. The cost of each money order—as high as 60 cents each—is usually set at a level aimed at discouraging their use in lieu of checks. In fact, unless the purchaser wants a relatively large amount of money converted into a money order, he or she might do better purchasing a postal money order, costing 30 cents for up to $300. Money orders are designed primarily for use by people who do not have bank accounts. Their cost might be high enough to encourage you to open an account.

For all of those monetary instruments that are as good

as cash, the bank service charge should only cover costs and not provide a profit. Regular bank customers should make it a point of determining if some or all of them are provided free.

And Away You Go

Banks make a big point of offering travelers checks as part of their package plans. Generally, they advertise that the customer can obtain travelers checks without paying the usual service charge. That can mean a savings of $1 for each $100 worth of checks purchased.

The willingness of banks to throw in the purchase fee for travelers checks indicates both that many people seldom, if ever, buy them and that banks can do without the service charge.

With the advent of the credit card, the need for carrying travelers checks has been reduced. Thus, the potential account holder should determine just how much of an actual savings can be realized from a package plan. Unlike a credit card, where the bank in effect grants you an advance, travelers checks are based on the customer's giving the bank a cash advance. Issuing banks make a big profit on the "float"—the funds that people have paid to purchase travelers checks that they have not yet cashed. Until the travelers check is used and returns to the issuing bank, the bank can use the purchaser's money for other purposes. In the New York area survey, only one bank provided travelers checks free. Actually there is no reason why a bank should charge a fee for checks it issues. New York's Citibank both issues travelers checks and charges a fee, probably so that it will not undercut other banks that also sell Citibank checks. It admits that 10 cents out of every $1 fee is profit, in addition to the interest income on the "float." Other banks, which do not have their own travelers checks, indicate a similar profit margin. Chase Manhattan and other banks that sell American Express travelers checks keep 67 cents of every $1 fee.

Barclay's Bank offered free travelers checks, even to those who are not its customers. Barclay's, a British-based bank, provides its own travelers checks.

Even if they don't issue their own checks, banks can make money by using the funds used to purchase them. They can reinvest those funds before they pass them on to the issuer of the checks. In short, travelers checks can be moneymakers for the bank, and the fee is just the icing on the cake. If you're a frequent user of travelers checks, it's worth shopping around. Many of the holding companies that own banks, like Citicorp in New York, or American Security in Washington, have travel agencies, and if you use a bank's own agency, it's worth asking for free travelers checks in return for doing business there. After all, the travel agency is also getting a commision on each ticket it sells.

Play It Safe

Every bank must have a vault in which to store its own cash. As an extra service, designed to attract customers, almost all banks make space available within the vault for safe deposit. Usually, safe-deposit boxes are not available to people who do not have accounts.

This is one service that is of far greater benefit to the customer than to the bank. In fact, virtually all banks lose money on the operation of their safe-deposit vault for customers. The average annual loss by big banks amounts to almost $6 per box per year.

The customer, on the other hand, has a safe place to leave important papers and other valuables, although they are not accessible except during banking hours. They may also be difficult to get at in case of the death of the box holder, because the Internal Revenue Service will want to know the contents of the box before it can be emptied. The IRS also offers an advantage to the box holder: the annual cost is usually tax deductible for those people who itemize deductions.

The only hitch is that a safe-deposit box is not quite so safe as most customers think. Of course, a lot less can happen to your valuables in a safe-deposit box than under the mattress, but if something happens to them in either place, you're a loser.

Thieves "dropped in" to the vault of the United California Bank at Laguna Niguel once, and walked off with the contents of 451 safe-deposit boxes. The property owners claimed they were out some $5 million and asked the bank to make good. The bank pointed to the fine print, which limited its liability to "the exercise of ordinary care" and included the understanding that "under no circumstances shall the lessor be liable for the loss or destruction of any other property, including money, placed in said safe."

Personal insurance policies may cover some or all of the contents. Aetna Life and Casualty offers a special policy for safe-deposit box holders.

When banks promote safe-deposit boxes, they stress safety and convenience. Both are relative, as United California's customers found out.

At Your Service

Many banks offer a variety of other services worth inquiring about. For example, the Bank of America has a special student account called the College Plan. Students pay only a $1-a-month service charge during the academic year and nothing during June, July, and August or when they maintain a minimum balance of $300. Scenic and personalized checks are available at low cost. Obviously, the College Plan is an excellent way to attract new customers.

Senior citizens also get special treatment by many banks. The advantage to the customer is the lower fees charged. The bank hopes for arrangement of automatic deposit of Social Security or pension checks and recognizes that many senior citizens use their checking accounts less often than younger people. The New York area survey indicates that small banks offer senior citizen accounts far more frequently than large banks.

Where either student accounts or senior citizen accounts do not exist, organized groups in a community may be able to convince a local bank to institute them.

The First National Bank of Lake Forest, Illinois, has provided for over sixty years a multiple-payee check. This enables customers to pay a number of bills by writing a single check, which is actually a payment order sent to the bank. The bank then deposits the proper amount in the accounts of the business firms or sends them a cashier's check on the date specified.

The multiple-payee check has real advantages for both the customer and the businesses, which find funds deposited to their accounts faster than usual. And it reduces the flow of paperwork caused by processing many separate checks, thus cutting bank costs. The bank may attract additional accounts in this way. This system is now being more widely introduced under the same terms as banking by phone.

Another service operated by Chemical Bank but available to other banks is the Braille Checking Account, which makes it possible for the blind to handle their own financial affairs.

A young couple is standing in line waiting to buy movie tickets. Suddenly they realize that they have no cash. The man sprints for a nearby Chemical Bank Cash Machine, inserts a card, receives cash, and sprints back, just in time to buy the tickets. This New York television commercial is a plug for an automated teller unit. These units will probably be heavily promoted in the future. But when it was first offered, you didn't immediately find out that there is both an annual $3 fee and a 25-cent-per-withdrawal charge. In addition, withdrawals are only possible in the amounts of $25 or $50. What would happen if the moviegoer only had $20 in the account?

In Nebraska, customers checking out at the supermarket can use an automatic teller unit to withdraw needed funds from their savings account. That's just the beginning of what these units will be able to do.

Some major banks act as paying agents for municipal or corporate bonds. All the customer has to do is arrange to collect the funds payable in person or by mail. If he happened to live near one of these banks, he would do well to stop in on the payment date. Otherwise, the bank can hold on to the funds for a few days, and the interest goes to the bank, not the customer.

If you have an account at a thrift institution or credit union, it may have a special arrangement with a commercial bank that could reduce service charges. For example, the Kansas Credit Union League has recently purchased the State Bank of Lancaster, Kansas. This alliance will allow credit unions, normally just a place for savings and consumer loans, to provide free checking, credit lines secured by credit-union balances, credit cards, and overdraft accounts. In New York, the mutual savings banks can extend the scope of their services through the Savings Bank Trust Company, which they own. It's always worth asking at a thrift if it has any special arrangements with another kind of banking institution.

Finally, banks provide an additional form of identification—a bank-identification or check-guarantee card for use in a world that seems to thrive on numbers and signatures as a sign of trust. At Citibank, these cards allow the customer to find out his account balance by inserting the card in a special machine. In large cities, where big banks have many branches they serve as identification in any branch when a customer wants to cash a check, usually of $100 or less. That saves time. In addition, a check-guarantee card tells any merchant that the bank vouches for the check up to $1,000. Of course, the banks will issue such a card only to customers who do not overdraw. The card may be useful as identification for other purposes, particularly if it bears a photograph.

The Fine Print

When the average customer opens a checking account, he or she generally knows little about the terms and conditions governing such an account. Most banks claim they make full information available in the brochures they leave in their main banking lobbies. Of course, many customers don't even examine these brochures, because they choose a bank on the basis of convenience and on the presumption that all banks are pretty much alike. Indeed, banks do not expect potential customers actually to shop around for an account by picking up the brochures from several banks and comparison-shopping. One man was told by Citibank that all checking account information was contained in the brochures, but when he went through a branch picking them up, he was first eyed suspiciously by the guard and then followed until he left.

Close examination of the checking account brochure picked up at Citibank revealed that it did not answer certain important questions. The brochure accentuates the positive and eliminates the negative. There is no mention of how the bank treats overdrawn checks. What fees are charged when checks deposited bounce? How is an inactive account defined, and what are the maintenance costs of such an account? What is the cost of a stop-payment order? Does the bank have the right to withdraw money from the account without the consent and possibly without the knowledge of the customer?

What is true for Citibank is also true of most other banks. Brochures are designed to attract customers, not to inform them of the drawbacks connected with opening a checking account. Obviously, banks believe that people need not become aware of some of the hidden costs until some time after their funds are on deposit. Among the major exceptions to this general rule of nondisclosure is the Bank of America, which grew to its great size as a consumer-oriented bank. It publishes a brochure called "The Facts," which explains the advantages and then some of the costs of its accounts. The brochure refers to "what to expect from normal use of your account." It also explains what happens when "not-so-normal" situations arise.

Offset, sometimes called the "banker's lien," is perfectly legal. The bank may withdraw from your checking account those funds needed to cover a debt to the bank, usually an outstanding installment or credit-card loan. The bank requires no court order, and it need not inform you that it has this right or that it is making use of it. Of course, an unknown withdrawal from your checking account can cause you to overdraw your balance unwittingly.

While a customer may not like the idea of offset, it is perfectly legal and avoidable. All the customer need do is keep his checking account in a different bank from the one where he borrows money, or avoid borrowing beyond what can easily be paid back. The bank will continually urge the customer to borrow more, so abstinence will, as usual, require willpower.

The main problem is in the failure of banks to disclose what they can or will do.

Citibank says it does not put this information on checking account forms, but does include it on the loan agreement. Offset is used only on loans more than 90 days overdue, and the bank attempts to warn the customer first.

Most banks appear not to include information about offset when a checking account is opened and do not plan to change their policy on this matter.

Of course, any bank may have to comply with a court order relating to funds they hold in your name (and also the contents of a safe-deposit box). Almost none will tell you in advance if they will levy a charge. The Bank of America says it will charge your checking account $7 if any such order is processed.

Everybody runs the risk of depositing a check to his or her account that is returned for one of a variety of reasons, most often because of insufficient funds. Indeed, the possibility of this happening is one reason given by banks for delaying in crediting funds to your account. Some banks will charge for the extra work involved in processing a return item; almost none will tell you they do. The Bank of America says it may charge 50 cents an item.

Of course, you may write a check that "bounces." Unless you know you're doing that at the time, overdrawing may be due to the failure of the bank to credit a deposit in the time you thought adequate. If you shave the margin thinly on a regular basis, just how long the bank requires for clearing and crediting is of vital importance.

Once a customer has overdrawn, the bank has two options. It may choose to process the check anyway. If the check is relatively small and if you generally maintain a good balance and ordinarily don't write bad checks, chances are that the bank will accept the overdraft. In the New York area survey, half of the big Manhattan banks said they would notify a customer before bouncing a check. That would give him time to increase his balance. Chances are pretty good that many banks will act without contacting the customer.

The bank may choose to reject the check, in which case it's sent back to the person the customer paid with it. That relieves the bank of any collection problems.

In either case, the bank will levy a fee for handling an overdrawn check. All banking surveys indicate that charges range from $2 to $5. They may be waived in certain cases. For example, Chase Manhattan says it does not charge the first time a customer errs and will waive charges for certain customers. A small mid-Western bank will charge $2 for the first overdraft on a given day and $1 each for all others on that day.

Many customers are unhappy about overdraft charges, particularly when they appear to be unjustified because they are based on delayed check clearance or unknown withdrawals from the account. Accounts that allow for overdrafts have been created, but they are, in fact, high-interest loans.

Another checking account feature is the stop-payment order. You may write a check and then decide that you should not have written it. In that case, you will ask your bank to stop payment. If the check has not yet returned to the bank and been debited from your account, the bank can issue an order for which it may charge. The cost ranges from nothing, where competition among banks is sharp, to $5. The order may be ineffective, even if issued in time. If you write a check to a merchant and he endorses it over to another party instead of depositing it, the innocent third party may well be able to collect from your account. In the case of a bank with many branches, even another branch of your own bank can be that innocent third party. Only the Bank of America among those surveyed explains this feature to potential account holders.

Finally, you may simply not use your account very much, even though you have left a small balance in it. The bank is incurring very few costs, if any. But many banks levy a charge that is supposed to cover their costs. The Bank of America charges $1 per month. In some states, if the account remains inactive, the funds are turned over to the state. This applies to both savings and checking accounts. With proper identification, they may be retrieved later.

All of these hidden charges cannot always be uncovered merely by reading the brochures banks make available or even by asking personnel. The bank regards the signature card that is used when an account is opened as a contract but it is unusually vague for a legal document. More often than not, the card will simply refer to the bank's rules and regulations and not include details of what the account might cost the customer. Whatever the card says, it's usually difficult for the account holder to get a copy of it. And if the potential customer doesn't like what he reads while sitting on the platform, how likely is it that he will simply walk away? That makes shopping for a checking account complicated if not occasionally embarrassing.

Check It Out

1. The first thing a potential checking account customer should do is make up a list of questions, **not** for the bank, but for himself or herself. Only by determining what you want from a checking account can you determine which checking account is best.

Here are some of the questions:

Do I write enough checks each month to require a checking account?

How many checks will I average each month?

How much money am I likely to have in the account at any one time?

Will deposits be fairly regular?

Do I use travelers checks? How much and how often?

Do I need a safe-deposit box?

Do I qualify (as a student or senior citizen) for a special account?

How often do I need or want to receive a statement?

Do I deposit many out-of-town checks to my account?

Am I likely to overdraw the account or stop payment?

Do I have a savings account in an institution that has links with a commercial bank?

2. Having answered these questions for yourself, it's time to ask banks a few questions. You can ask your questions by phone or in person. You're likely to get fuller answers in person, but you have to be willing to spend a few minutes. Chances are you will have to speak with a senior person on the platform, if not the branch manager. Some banks will be more cooperative than others. Since your mental well-being is at least as important as your financial well-being, how you are treated should influence your choice of a bank.

Ask these questions and write down the answers:

In choosing an account:

What are the service charges of all accounts offered as well as the per-check charges, the required minimum or average balance (if any, and what interest income is lost), and the cost of checks?

What is the comparative cost of accounts, given my circumstances? (If the bank won't help you figure this answer out, promise to return only after you have made such calculations for yourself.)

In deciding on a package plan:

What are the charges for travelers checks, safe-deposit boxes, certified and cashier's checks, and loans? (The value of these answers depends on how often you would use these services.)

In deciding on a bank:

What are the costs of overdrafts (and are you notified), returned checks, inactivity, stop-payment orders, and does the bank use offset?

What additional features are offered, like automated teller and multipayment checks, and what do they cost?

How frequently are statements provided?

What special accounts are offered?

Can I obtain immediate crediting for deposits of checks to be collected later?

3. Only when you have all the answers should you choose the bank for your account. There's no indication that you are likely to do better in obtaining the kind of checking account you want according to the size of the bank or part of the country in which it's located. Of course, the exceptions are those states in which NOW accounts are available. Competition appears to be a factor in all markets, but in many respects banking markets are isolated from each other. Of course, convenience is important, but if you can save several dollars a month by using a more distant bank, it may be wise to consider banking by mail. If a NOW or USA account appeals to you, consider the advantages of having two accounts.

4. It's more than possible that you will not get satisfactory answers to many of your questions from any bank. But banks are sensitive to public pressure and you may be able to organize with others to improve your chances of finding a bank that suits your needs. For example, a university student council could organize a drive for student checking accounts or a civic organization could muster support for senior citizen accounts. The organizing group should represent enough potential customers that local banks will listen to their demands.

3 No Saving Grace

Like a lot of other working men, Mike Pellegrino, a New York television news film editor, had always wanted to set some money aside for his kids. Finally, he saw a Citibank ad for "Golden Growth bonds." Attracted by the interest rate and the promise that interest would be paid from the day of deposit to the day of withdrawal, he opened an account. In the next week, he opened two more accounts, each with identical initial deposits.

Four years later, Mike went back to Citibank and cashed in each account on its anniversary. He was amazed to receive three different amounts in return for the accounts, because they had all held the same basic deposit for exactly the same period. When he questioned a bank officer, Mike ran into a stone wall. Months later, he was still waiting for a promised explanation.

Mike's case illustrates two of the most important characteristics of bank savings. First, he was attracted to Citibank by its advertising and its convenience to the place he worked. Second, neither he, the depositor, nor the bank officials fully understood the rules governing his savings accounts. About the only untypical aspect of this case was Mike's persistence in trying to find out why he had not received the same return on identical accounts.

People save money in a lot of ways. They put their extra money into the stock market, United States Savings Bonds, Treasury securities, municipal bonds, pension funds, life insurance, money market funds, and gold. Obviously some of these investments represent more than simple savings.

Investments, such as those in common stock, may offer the best hedge against inflation, because they tend to grow as the economy grows, but they offer little security, since they may slump substantially when the economy slows down. Savings in a bank means less growth than is possible in the good times on the stock market but absolute security of the amount saved. That's why most saving takes place in commercial banks and in thrift institutions—savings banks or savings and loan associations.

Banks, Thrifts, and Accounts

More people save at commercial banks than at any other institutions, because they are convenient and offer one-stop shopping for banking needs. But commercial banks usually pay lower interest than thrift institutions. Commercial banks come in all shapes and sizes—and kinds. Much depends on what government agency regulates them—state or Federal—and whether they are insured by the Federal Deposit Insurance Corporation (FDIC), by a state agency, or not at all. Almost all commercial banks are insured by the FDIC. Don't put your money in a noninsured bank; it offers far less security than an insured bank.

Government regulators allow commercial banks to provide a wide variety of savings accounts. Technically, money placed in an interest-bearing account that may be withdrawn without advance notice is called a savings deposit. Money that can be withdrawn with interest after a fixed period of time is known as a time deposit. Under government rules, set by the Federal Reserve, maturities on time deposits are 30 to 89 days, 90 days to 1 year, 1 to 2½ years, 2½ or more years, 4 to 6 years, and 6 years and above. As we'll see, these periods are tied to interest rates in such a way as to ensure that savers who are willing to leave their funds with the bank for longer periods will receive higher rates of interest. By setting such rules, Federal authorities regulate competition to protect smaller banks from being driven out of business, thus reducing consumer choice. Often, banks themselves will impose a maximum length on any open-ended periods in order to avoid being locked into paying a high rate of interest at a time when interest rates may again have fallen.

These account periods relate to amounts of less than $100,000. For the big customers, the Federal Reserve Board, a regulatory agency for all national and some state banks, may well choose not to set any restrictions and simply let the bank and the customer negotiate terms. Generally, on such large accounts, banks offer very high rates for short-term deposits but do not want to promise high payments long into the future.

After commercial banks, most people favor savings and loan associations. They, too, are subject to a dual state-Federal system of regulation. Just as the Federal Reserve is responsible for commercial banks, the Federal Home Loan Bank Board (FHLB) watches the savings and loans. At the end of 1975, there were 2,916 state-chartered savings and loans and 2,048 Federally chartered savings and loans.

Federal associations are required to have their deposits insured by the Federal Savings and Loan Insurance Corporation (FSLIC), an institution similar to the FDIC. In addition, state associations may obtain such insurance, and many do. In three states—Massachusetts, Ohio, and Maryland—state insurance plans are used instead of FSLIC.

At most savings and loans, if you're a depositor, you're a part owner. Some savings and loans are owned by shareholders, as are almost all commercial banks (except those few individually owned). That means they must use some of their income to pay dividends to shareholders.

Like most commercial banks, savings and loan associations are now authorized to provide a wide variety of savings accounts. Until 1966, setting rates and kinds of accounts was strictly up to association managers. As a result, they often set rates so that the associations were at a competitive advantage in relation to commercial and mutual savings banks. In those days, California savings and loans, paying high interest, actively advertised for customers, even in the New York newspapers. Because savings and loans must dedicate their deposits to home mortgage loans, government policy favoring as much housing construction as possible meant that they were given preference in the money market.

After 1966, Federal regulators placed limits on the interest rates that the associations could offer. In part, these limits reflected concern that the associations would push rates higher than would be wise for their own long-term stability. They might offer high rates but have too many low-rate mortgages to be able to meet their own interest bill. The ceilings did not reduce the savings and loans' ability to attract savings, because of their established positions in their communities and the slightly higher interest that they may offer as compared with commercial banks.

Savings and loans offer regular passbook accounts and a number of time-deposit arrangements. These include 90-day accounts, 90- to 179-day, 180- to 364-day, 1- to 2-year, and 2- to 10-year accounts, each with a progressively higher interest rate.

Because the chief purpose of savings and loan associations is to provide funds for the home mortgage market, those who save at savings and loans are better off if they turn to the same association for a mortgage loan. While they will not get preferential rates, their own credit will already have been, in part, established. Merely having left funds with a savings and loan over a period of a year or more will indicate a degree of stability in managing your affairs that will please a potential lender.

Savings and loans lack the convenience of the many-branched commercial banks, which are spread across the face of the land in great profusion. Almost half of the associations are located in Pennsylvania, Illinois, Ohio, New Jersey, Texas, Maryland, and California.

Mutual savings banks, the third-ranking type of banking institution for savings deposits, are even less widely spread. There are 475 of them, located in seventeen states and Puerto Rico. Well more than half of these are located in Massachusetts and New York, with all but a handful located in New England, New York, and New Jersey. They're likely to be larger institutions than savings and loans: The assets of the average savings bank are likely to be greater than those of the average savings and loan association.

Deposits in these banks are insured by the FDIC, in most cases, or by state insurance funds, notably one in Massachusetts. Only one mutual savings bank is not insured.

Although the Federal Reserve Board keeps tabs on them, the mutual savings banks are state regulated. As their name implies, these banks are owned by their depositors. But as with corporate stock ownership, people with savings accounts are hardly in a position to set corporate policy.

Because most savings banks are members of the FDIC, they are subject to Federally imposed interest-rate ceilings. Until savings and loan associations were placed under similar regulation, the mutual savings banks generally offered lower rates of interest. Recently, however, savers have found the same array of savings choices at the same interest rates available in both kinds of institutions.

As with the savings and loans, savings bank customers have a built-in advantage should they wish to borrow money from a bank where they have an account. If the customer seeks a mortgage, he is already known by the bank. A fully secured loan on the pledge of a passbook is easy to obtain and available at about as reasonable a rate as possible. The advantage of a passbook loan is that you do not dissipate your savings but instead pay for a purchase out of current income. Your funds continue to earn interest, so the net interest cost is only the difference between the interest paid and the interest charged. The interest paid is deductible on income taxes. Such loans are easy to obtain. Finally, by using money in a savings account to guarantee a loan, you do not run the risk of losing any interest because of a withdrawal made before the end of the period during which you had promised to leave the money in the bank.

The smallest of the savings institutions in terms of deposits are the credit unions, but they are the fastest growing. Almost twenty-three thousand cover the country, with major concentrations in the largest states—California, Pennsylvania, Illinois, Ohio, and New York.

For the consumer, the chief distinction between credit unions and other savings institutions has been that he or she cannot just walk in off the street and open an account. Now, credit unions are increasingly open to all comers, not just those people who are affiliated with the sponsoring organization. Credit unions distribute any "profits" they make in the form of dividends to their members. Management is often voluntary rather than paid, with officers elected by the members. Of course, the larger credit unions have paid staffs.

Many of the credit unions are quite small, with more than half of them having assets of less than $500,000. They can be either Federally or state chartered, but both can obtain $40,000 per account deposit insurance from the National Credit Union Administration (NCUA). The NCUA acts as the Federal regulatory agency, while state banking departments supervise credit unions that they charter.

Credit unions are the odd birds among financial institutions. They are exempt from Federal income taxes, are not held to the same monetary reserve requirements as banks, and may have their operating costs subsidized by the host company or organization.

At this time, the credit unions are relatively limited in the services they can provide to their saver members, but this is changing. They generally offer one kind of account, with the interest ceiling set by the NCUA or state banking departments. This rate, for what amounts to accounts containing a minimum deposit for at least one quarter, usually exceeds rates payable on similar passbook accounts. For example, some credit unions offer 6 or 7 percent, while the highest bank rate on a 90-day savings account is 5.5 percent. A few issue credit union certificates as a way of raising additional funds for lending. Such certificates may be available even to non-members.

Members enjoy an absolute preference when it comes time to borrow relatively small amounts from credit unions. Perhaps the most frequent loan is for the purchase of an automobile. Credit unions can also make mortgage loans. In addition, credit unions provide life insurance on outstanding loans at no extra cost.

A Matter of Great Interest

Once a saver is able to sort out the various kinds of institutions and accounts, he or she will probably find the same account labeled in two different ways in two different banks. With interest rates so closely regulated, just about the only way one bank can attract savers as opposed to any other bank is through marketing. It's a case of putting basically the same product in a fancier package.

Savings accounts have all kinds of names, most of which do little to explain the nature of the account. It's up to the consumer to strip away the frills to determine which of the basic accounts is being offered.

In 1974, allowable rates were just about as high as they had ever been, reflecting tight-money policies and the willingness of banks and thrifts to bid high for the funds they needed to make loans. Of course, interest rates change often. But they tend to remain in the same general relation to each other, whatever their actual level.

The graph on page 59 indicates the general trend of the average annual rates of interest paid on savings accounts by commercial banks, savings and loan associations, and mutual savings banks.

Two caveats ought to be kept in mind in reading this graph. First, the commercial bank interest rate reflects both individual savings and big, high-yield accounts held by corporations and other large investors. Second, the chart indicates an average and thus reflects the preponderance of individual savers who choose the lowest-interest-bearing accounts, the ones from which they can withdraw their funds without any loss of interest and without advance notice.

Rules and Regulations

After July 1973, Federal regulatory agencies began to bring the variety of savings accounts into line, whatever the banking institution offering them. Top interest rates payable on a comparative basis are shown in the accompanying table.

Interest Rate Ceilings on Consumer-Type Savings and Time Deposits
(as of December 31, 1976)

	FDIC Mutual Savings	*FHLB Savings and Loan*	*FDIC Commercial*
Passbook accounts	5.25%	5.25%	5.00%
Time deposits maturing in:			
90 days to 1 year	5.75%	5.75%	5.50%
1 to 2½ years	6.50%	6.50%	6.00%
2½ to 4 years (minimum of $1,000 for certain Savings and Loans) *	6.75%	6.75%	6.50%
4 to 6 years (minimum of $1,000) *	7.50%	7.50%	7.25%
6 years or more (minimum of $1,000)	7.75%	7.75%	7.50%

* No minimum for IRA and Keogh plans.

The NCUA permits Federal credit unions to offer as much as 7 percent on their savings accounts, which are called share accounts because savers buy "shares" of the credit union and become part owners. The most frequently offered rate is 6 percent.

No such ceilings exist on "nonconsumer-type" savings deposits, those above $100,000. This distinction may look like a rather obvious attempt by the regulators to favor the rich, but actually the ceilings are dictated by conditions in the money market. This is the "market" where all those who want to borrow—business banks, governments, and individ-

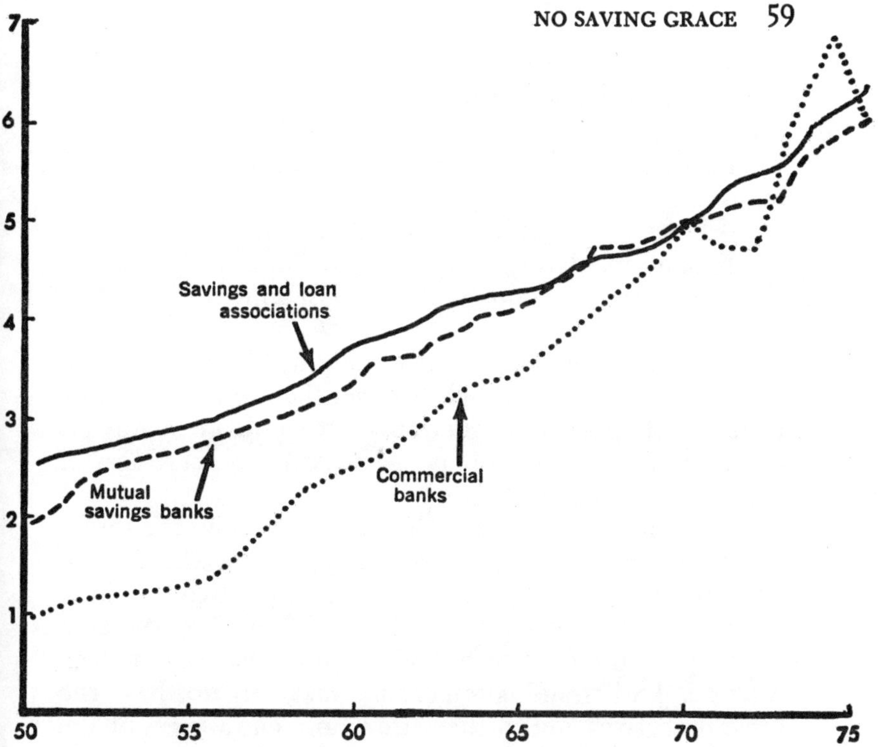

uals—"meet" all those who want to lend. It exists in no single place, but New York is its focal point. Generally, higher interest rates are offered in the market for larger amounts of money. It's easier to raise $100,000 from one person than from one hundred people, and it's reasonable that the one person should get some sort of financial reward resulting from the economy to the borrowing institution. Hence, a higher interest rate.

By 1973, big depositors were increasingly attracted by the higher interest rates they could obtain by purchasing United States Treasury bills like savings bonds but costing at least $10,000 and maturing in a period of months, and similar items in the money market, and the banks feared that they would lose their deposits. The regulators lifted the ceiling in order to let banks compete, and rates immediately rose from 6 percent to above 9 percent.

All this was of little interest to the average saver who would not have enough money to become a lender in the money market. When the regulators want to allow banks to attract funds from smaller savers, they authorize increases in the ceilings on deposits of less than $100,000. That's just what happened after the ceiling on larger deposits was removed.

When states have lower ceilings than those dictated by the Federal regulatory agencies, even those banks that are Federally chartered and regulated must adhere to the state ceiling.

Obviously, Federal rule makers want to keep commercial bank interest rates slightly lower than those offered by thrifts. Without this distinction, there would be no way for the savings and loans and savings banks to compete against the commercial banks.

The difference between the rates offered by the thrifts and by commercial banks is generally no more than ¼ of 1 percent. For accounts of one and one-half to two years, the gap widens to ½ of 1 percent. These differences may seem virtually meaningless at first glance, but they may not always be. Thrifts and commercial banks may not have the same objectives and so they stress different aspects of the rate structure. The thrifts lend out money for longer periods than the commercial banks so they seek longer-term deposits. As a result, they advertise the interest they pay on higher-rate, long-term accounts. Commercial banks, with shorter-term loans, push lower-interest, short-term savings accounts. Most savers put their money in the short-term accounts, where they are not committed to leave their funds. Many people who have checking accounts at commercial banks make the extra effort of going to a thrift to get the slightly higher interest for passbook accounts.

In short, the interest-rate differential, coupled with the banks' own needs for specific kinds of deposits, ensures customers for each kind of institution.

Why do the Federal authorities get involved in setting interest ceilings at all? Merely to protect certain kinds of institutions? Actually, putting different interest lids on savings accounts is designed to ensure that funds will be available for a variety of purposes, but most importantly for mortgages. Without controls, regulators fear, thrifts would offer too high rates of interest in order to attract more funds. But the income to pay these high rates would have to come from a mix of old and new mortgages. Given the low rates on older mortgages, income would not be sufficient to meet interest payments at levels to which they might freely float. Rates on new mortgages would have to move to even higher levels to compensate. Hence, ceilings on interest. And as we have seen, differentials are meant to provide funds for both consumer loans by commercial banks and mortgage loans, mostly by thrifts.

The Case of the "Wild Card"

Of course, either unforeseen circumstances or mistakes by regulators in setting ceilings can lead to savings flowing into the wrong kinds of accounts, at least in terms of national objectives. For example, this occurred for a few months during 1973.

In July 1973, commercial banks were allowed to pay any interest they wanted on four-year accounts with a minimum deposit of $1,000. In order to limit transfers of funds from traditional savings accounts to the new accounts, Federal regulators said that only 5 percent of a bank's time deposits could be in no-ceiling accounts. In some commercial banks, interest rates immediately took off. Chemical Bank New York Trust pegged its interest rate on these "Wild Card" accounts to the going rate for United States Treasury bills. Citibank set its rate one-half point below the prevailing prime rate—the short-term interest rate charged big borrowers with the highest credit ratings. But as an added inducement, the rate payable during the first quarter was set at an astronomical 10 percent, whatever the base rate did.

The "Wild Card" accounts suddenly allowed the small saver the same kind of potential gain that had been reserved for those saving more than $100,000. Obviously, there was more risk in a "Wild Card" account than in a traditional savings account because of the possible fluctuations in interest rates. To reassure savers, banks made interest floors a part of the arrangement. For example, Citibank set a 5-percent minimum and Chemical Bank set a 6-percent minimum, well above the passbook rate. On a four-year account, then being offered by the thrifts, the saver was guaranteed 7.5 percent.

Despite the element of risk on return, savers began withdrawing funds from savings banks and savings and loans to put into the fluctuating-interest accounts. This sudden transfer of funds out of thrifts is called disintermediation. In simple language, those banks losing accounts stopped playing their expected role as intermediaries between savers and borrowers. Some borrowers, notably those who needed mortgages, began to run into problems finding funds at the thrifts, because money was flowing to the commercial banks. At those banks, the new receipts were used to finance short-term loans on which it was possible to charge higher interest than on long-term mortgages. Higher interest income enabled the commercial banks to pay at a higher rate.

The Federal regulators had mistakenly calculated that higher interest rates at the commercial banks would draw more spending money into banks. They did not expect that most of the money going into "Wild Card" accounts would simply be coming out of other savings accounts. Perhaps, too, they did not expect the commercial banks to offer rates as high as 10 percent.

The thrifts were quick to move. They warned Congress that massive disintermediation, with a related reduction in mortgage money, was sure to result if the "Wild Card" accounts remained in effect. Within two days of the first alarm, a bill was introduced and passed that simply overruled the regulators and set a ceiling on four-year deposits at commercial banks. Thus ended the short history of interest-rate competition for small deposits among banks.

Even congressional action did not stop some banks from trying to offer higher rates. Instead of the banks themselves, their holding companies took the next step. In July 1974, Citicorp, which owns First National City Bank, marketed floating-rate notes. These issues promised to pay 9.7 percent interest until May 1975 and then interest at one point above the Treasury bill rate. After June 1976, purchasers could cash the notes in and receive the full purchase price.

Citicorp was promptly followed by seven other banks and two industrial corporations. Corporations? Yes, because the notes were not insured at all, as are bank deposits, since even the bank issues were technically made by corporations. The higher interest rate was in part compensation for the lack of insurance. Some $1.3 billion worth of floating-rate notes was sold in two months.

Three things happened that slowed and eventually stopped sales. First, Congress threatened legal action against the notes, unless they were made somewhat less attractive. As a result, the Federal Reserve was able to prevail upon Citicorp to make it somewhat more difficult to cash in the notes and not to guarantee the high return for a long period. Second, interest rates began to fall. Floating-rate notes are just that, and the interest paid can go down just as easily as it can go up. These notes looked a lot more attractive as rates rose than they did when they fell. At that point, an insured 7.5 percent account looked pretty good. Third, when Franklin National went broke, depositors with insurance were paid immediately. Anybody who held notes had to wait, like any other creditor, for the division of what was left. That did a lot to weaken enthusiasm for uninsured notes.

Congress and the Federal regulators have come to understand that their efforts to prevent disintermediation require full-time surveillance. Even the Treasury itself, in 1969 and again in 1974, issued high-interest paper that sopped up savings account money like a sponge. The first time it was a mistake and the Treasury acted to cut off the savings outflow. The second time was no mistake, for the Treasury was willing to pay high interest and attract savings account money at about the very same time it was trying to discourage the sale of floating-rate notes.

An Interest-Rate Menu

Of course, interest-rate maximums are just that—the most that the law will allow. No bank or savings institution is required to pay interest at those rates. Competitive conditions in a particular market will determine the interest rates that will be offered. Most institutions operate on the theory that the saver will not wander outside his immediate home market, thus relieving them of any obligation to offer rates competitive with those available elsewhere. Some undoubtedly believe that because of convenience and perhaps market domination, they can afford to offer lower rates without losing deposits.

Look, for example, at Citibank, the second-largest bank in the nation, which is located in the heart of the highly competitive New York City market. Here's what it offered in 1977. On a passbook account, Citibank offered 4.5 percent and only provided the maximum 5 percent if the saver was willing to accept a statement, similar to a checking account statement, instead of having each transaction entered in his or her passbook. Citibank says that it saves on expenses this way.

Citibank's Regular Golden Passbook Account allowed withdrawals at the end of each calendar quarter or on 90 days' written notice. In line with interest-rate regulations, it would not pay 5.5 percent interest unless the money was left on deposit for at least 90 days. The minimum deposit was $500, an amount not required by regulation. The Special Golden Passbook offers 6 percent for deposits of at least one year. The minimum deposit was one year.

Next step up the ladder was the Premium Golden Passbook Account, which was offered for a minimum of 2½ years at the maximum allowable rate of 6.5 percent. Again, the minimum deposit, not required by regulation, was $500. The saver had to pick his own maturity date. Finally, the Investment Golden Passbook offered 7.25 percent on deposits of at least $1,000 left with the bank for at least 4 years. The minimums in the case were set by federal regulation. He was, in fact, betting that interest rates would decline later, and especially after the seventh year. Over the long run, rates don't usually come down, but the precipitous climb in recent years allows for some expectation that they'll fall again.

Many commercial banks offer completely different varieties of savings accounts. Almost none is likely to provide the full range of savings choices at the maximum rates allowable by law. Indeed, a random sample of small-town commercial banks indicates that they tend to offer fewer of the high-interest accounts. With relatively small assets, they simply cannot afford to commit themselves to pay a high rate of interest over a long period of time. As a result, they will offer passbook accounts at the lowest interest rate the market will allow.

At the end of 1975, savings and loan associations were paying an average interest rate about one-quarter of a point higher than commerical banks. This lead reflected the higher passbook rate they were allowed to pay (5 percent as opposed to 4.5 percent) and the willingness of savers at the associations to leave their money in accounts paying a higher rate of interest.

But like commercial banks, savings and loans do not always pay at the maximum allowable. A case in point was the Home Savings and Loan Association of Los Angeles, the largest in the nation and located in an area where most of the association giants operate. While it offered passbook and time-deposit accounts at the legal maximums in 1974, a time when banks were aggressively seeking savers, it offered no 7.5 percent, 4-year accounts on amounts of $1,000 or more as authorized by federal regulation. So you would have missed the highest available rates if you had wanted, for example, to deposit $2,000 for five years. Later, Home fell into line with other thrifts and was fully competitive.

Smaller savings and loans follow the same conservative pattern as the smaller commercial banks.

The largest mutual savings banks, many of which are located in New York City, break the pattern. They usually offer interest rates at the maximums allowable by law. On accounts other than passbook or the highest-interest accounts where a $1,000 minimum is required by regulation, the mutual savings banks require a minimum deposit of $500 in the account at all times.

Once again, smaller savings banks tend to offer fewer high-interest accounts. Of two banks in Vermont, for example, which operate in different markets, one provided the full range of accounts at the maximums, while another would pay no more than 5.5 percent on a 90-day account.

Perhaps as a reflection of the savings orientations of consumers in various parts of the country, the average interest rate paid by savings banks, concentrated in the East, was almost a fifth of a point lower than in savings and loans, concentrated in the West.

As for credit unions, they operate under a flat ceiling. The top interest rate they can pay is 7 percent. A national survey indicated that a great many of them paid substantially less than the maximum. In some cases, state law sets the maximum a full point below the federally permitted level. In a few states, credit unions charted by the state can pay more than the federal maximum.
Michigan—the maximum rate was 5 percent.

The applicable maximum interest rate permitted in 1977 was 7 percent. In the face of climbing interest rates, more credit unions moved toward higher payouts. For those few large credit unions that offer certificates, the interest rates may go as much as a point higher than the allowable maximum payment for share accounts. Maturities on these certificates range from those that were redeemable at any time after issue to those that must be held one year. Thus, they may, where available, amount to the most attractive savings choice available, because they combine high interest and relatively short maturity.

When the potential saver is faced with the impressive publicity each of these institutions puts out in an attempt to attract his or her money, there are a few items in the fine print that are worth watching closely.

The Rock Bottom

As already indicated, many of the higher-interest-paying accounts require that a minimum deposit be kept in the account at all times in order for the account to be kept open at all. These minimums are generally on the order of $500 or $1,000. Even a regular passbook account at a savings bank may require $25 to $100 in the account in order for interest to be paid, although the account may be kept open with a lesser amount. When the interest already due on a day-of-deposit–day-of-withdrawal account is not paid until the end of a quarter, the saver must be careful to keep the required minimum in the account for that time in order to get the interest already due. So it's important for a saver to know exactly how much will have to be committed to any savings plan, keeping in mind that at some time in the future he or she may want to make an unplanned withdrawal. If such a withdrawal would bring the balance in the account down below the minimum required for payment of a high interest rate, you were unwise to choose it in the first place.

Minimum deposits get tricky when it comes to adding money to an account of a fixed maturity that is already open. The saver cannot add to an existing account and expect to have the additional deposit treated the same way as the initial deposit unless he or she extends the life of the entire account. For example, an executive who thought he would put his extra cash into a 90-day account at the savings bank in order to receive 5.75 percent interest, came back a month after opening the account with an additional deposit. He was barred from simply adding his second deposit, even on the commitment that he would leave that deposit with the bank for 30 days beyond the first one. He was told that he either had to extend the first deposit to a 120-day account or meet the minimum to open an entirely new account for the second deposit. That's why banks may call anything beyond a passbook account a savings certificate or bond or certificate of deposit, because, in most cases, time requirements make it virtually impossible to add to an existing account.

Paying the Penalty

Federal regulators have attached high penalties to the premature withdrawal of principal from a high-interest savings account. Banks can afford to promise high interest only on the understanding that they will have the saver's money over a definite period—usually a relatively long one. That way the banks can be certain to commit their funds to loans that will cover the cost of the depositor's interest. In short, the reason higher interest is paid is that the depositor is willing to leave the money for a predetermined period. From the depositor's viewpoint, if interest rates decline later, it was a wise move to get the money tied up in a high-interest account for a long period.

Of course, some people have to lay their hands on their savings at short notice. Anybody can withdraw the interest already earned and paid without any hindrance whatsoever. But such a withdrawal will reduce the effective yield of the account, which is calculated on the basis of both principal and accrued interest's being left on deposit until the account runs its course.

All banks are required to inform the depositor in advance about the penalties attached to early withdrawal. On some older accounts, most of which have been closed, the depositor had to prove to the bank's satisfaction that the withdrawal was made necessary by dire personal circumstances, like a death in the family. Later the regulators retreated from imposing such strenuous terms. Now, almost no bank will refuse to permit the withdrawal, although it must exact the penalty.

Publicity for savings accounts must include the disclaimer describing the penalty. If it is couched in the official regulator's language, the depositor is going to find it tough to understand just what toll is exacted for early withdrawal. Some banks provide examples in their promotional literature of just how much the early withdrawal fee would be.

Here's how the penalty works. The interest rate paid on the amount withdrawn is not the high rate originally offered, but the passbook rate provided by the institution during the time the money was on deposit. Thus, in a savings bank, if a person takes money out of a 6.75-percent account, the interest payable on that money is 5.25 percent. Of course, the saver must leave in the account an amount greater than the required minimum deposit. Otherwise the entire account is closed by the withdrawal. Then, the interest that is to be paid on the amount withdrawn, at the reduced rate, is further cut by a total forfeit of three months' worth of interest. For an example of an actual loss, Home Savings and Loan of Los Angeles provides this case:

Example of Penalty on a 6.75-Percent Account

If $1,000 is withdrawn one year after the account was opened, the penalty would be $28.45.

The penalty is based on the following calculations:

1. Loss of one year's interest at 6.75 percent	$68.08
2. Payment of nine months' interest at 5.25 percent	39.63
3. Total penalty loss	$28.45

Some banks may insist that they have the right to refuse a withdrawal even with these penalty provisions. If the saver contemplates the possibility of a premature withdrawal, he or she should discuss the matter in advance, and if in any remaining doubt, get a statement in writing that he or she will be able to make the withdrawal. Despite their strict statements, designed to discourage early withdrawals, most banks will, in fact, permit them.

Making a person who has left funds in the account for a considerable period pay the same penalty as a person who has withdrawn funds earlier in the planned life of the account strikes some as unfair. After all, the bank has enjoyed the use of the funds for a considerable period and ought to pay for that use. One way would be to pay interest according to the duration funds were actually left in the account. This method would not require a decision in advance by the saver on just how long he or she would leave funds in the account. Freyda Koplow, the former Massachusetts banking commissioner, proposed a variation on this scheme by allowing the saver to decide at the start of each year whether he or she will leave funds in the account at a high interest rate.

What Happens Next?

What if the saver leaves his funds in the account beyond the maturity date? Banks and thrifts should tell the depositor, before the account is opened, what will happen to the deposit in this case, but many don't so it's wise to ask. The least desirable possibility is that the institution will simply hang on to the money without paying any interest at all. Without contrary advice from the depositor, that's what the Federal Reserve requires its commercial bank members to do. Some institutions will automatically place the funds on deposit in a passbook account, thus assuring at least a minimal rate of interest. Generally, this will allow the customer to withdraw the money whenever he or she wishes, although the saver may be required to wait until the end of a quarter and to avoid losing any interest. Other savings institutions have automatic "roll-over" provisions, which means that the funds on deposit will be placed again in exactly the same kind of account they were in, provided that kind of account is still available. The danger here is that the depositor may not want to have his or her funds tied up again for a considerable period of time. A good bank will notify the depositor well in advance of the termination date of the account and offer all alternatives, including payment of all the proceeds to the depositor. A good saver will keep records, permitting prompt action to reinvest funds most profitably.

Guaranteed Return

The higher-interest-rate accounts "guarantee" the rate until the specified maturity. But since interest-rate maximums are subject to government regulation, can't one of the regulatory agencies require that the rate be lowered at any time? In fact, there is nothing that would prevent an agency from doing just that, except for the inevitable public outcry. Thus, in order to maintain public confidence in savings institutions and in their inducements to attract savings, it is virtually inconceivable that such an action would be taken.

But savers should be careful to see if, in fact, they are being guaranteed an interest rate. If "interest" is called "dividends" on the passbook account they open, no return is certain. Dividends are payable on earnings. Mutual savings banks pay dividends, not interest, on their passbook accounts. Both are careful to tell customers that the interest rates they are paying at the moment a deposit is made is only the anticipated rate for the future. In recent years, these rates have gone above anticipated levels, but they can go down just as easily. High-interest accounts are not usually subject to fluctuation, but rates on passbook accounts can be adjusted. If they do change, the rate is adjusted automatically, and there is no need for the depositor to open a new account.

A Member of the Club

Christmas Clubs and similar devices have always been the stepchildren of savings. For a long period, banks paid no interest at all on deposits made by individuals seeking to save up enough to pay for Chirstmas presents. That practice is virtually ended, but there are still "costs" to savers who continue to participate. Presumably, the additional paperwork of preparing coupon booklets and posting the number of the payment due each week justifies these "costs."

Most important, the depositor is almost always required to complete all payments to the club before any annual interest is paid. Obviously, banks want to make sure their administrative expense is justified before they pay for the use of savers' money. In that case, savings banks will often pay interest at the same rate as the passbook account. Commercial banks may offer less. For example, some commercial banks in New York pay 5 percent on passbook accounts but only 4.5 percent on Christmas/Chanukah clubs. In some cases, banks will pay higher interest to people who have funds transferred automatically from their checking accounts to the clubs than they pay to coupon rippers.

Banks report that the clubs actually cost them money. Each club member makes about thirty-five deposits a year, more than the average saver. And a great number of accounts are opened and closed each year, unlike savings accounts, which may remain open for extended periods. But banks find that the clubs are one way of attracting customers and a competitive device that they must maintain simply because others do.

The interest paid on club accounts averages about 3 percent, a sure indication that some banks pay little or no interest and many depositors do not keep up their payments regularly. One missed week, and all the interest for the year is lost.

Clearly, unless the saver is so weak-willed as to require constant reminders provided by the club, he or she is far better off placing funds regularly in a passbook account. The bank will probably be happier, too. Of course, the saver has to be able to withstand the temptation of taking money out of the account before there is enough on hand to pay for gifts. Interest may well be paid both on the money withdrawn and on the money left in a passbook account, while all interest may stop when any withdrawal is made from a club.

For Retiring People

Anyone saving for retirement can use his or her bank's savings accounts to set up a plan with definite tax advantage. A so-called Keogh Plan covers self-employed people, and an Individual Retirement Account (IRA) is designed for people whose employers do not have a pension plan that covers them.

You can withdraw money from your current income, lock it into a retirement plan, and not have to pay taxes on that income now. You are expected to leave that money in the plan until you reach the age of 59½. If not, you pay a 10 percent tax penalty on the amount you withdraw, plus income taxes on that amount. If you leave the funds alone until your retirement, principal and dividends are only taxed as they are withdrawn, almost certainly at a time when your reduced income has put you in a lower tax bracket than when you contributed to the plan.

Under the Keogh Plan, each year you can place 15 percent of your self-employment income into the Plan, but no more than $7,500. If you earn $750 to $5,000, you can put $750 into the Plan, even though that's more than 15 percent. You may put up to 15 percent of salary or $1,500, whichever is less, into an IRA. Beginning in 1977, you could deposit up to $1,750 (or 15 percent) if you have a nonworking spouse. But you and your mate must both have IRAs and $875 must be contributed to the Plan of each, if the full $1,750 is to be deposited and deducted from taxes. If you contribute more than is allowed to either plan, the excess is subject to an annual 6 percent excise tax, payable each year the excess remains in the account. And, if you withdraw the surplus to avoid paying the 6 percent excise in the future, you must pay the 10 percent extra tax on an early withdrawal.

While you may establish a Keogh Plan or IRA in stocks and bonds or through an insurance company, the most secure plan and almost certainly the least expensive in terms of handling charges is probably at a bank or thrift. You may wait to make your deposit until February 15 or the year following the tax year involved (assuming it ends on December 31) in order to be sure just how much you want to deposit, so as to avoid penalties on excess contributions and to measure the impact of the tax savings. Deposits need not be made on a regular schedule.

The saver should make sure that he or she gets the best rate possible. Until 1977, depositors were governed by the rules relating to usual savings accounts, including minimum deposits and deposit periods. The federal regulators announced that both commercial banks and thrifts could pay up to 7.75 percent interest on Keogh Plans and IRAs. There is no minimum deposit, although the accounts must remain for a minimum three year period. Obviously, the removal of the deposit minimum gives small depositers a major interest rate boost.

For anyone saving for retirement anyway or looking for a way to reduce federal income taxes, a Keogh Plan or IRA at a bank may be a very good deal. Because the rules are relatively complicated, it's a good idea to inquire at the bank well before the deposit deadline to find out about interest rates and other conditions.

The Three Cs

Interest rates should be expected to tell the whole story about where to put your money. But things are seldom what they seem. Even the banks themselves tell the saver that the effective annual yield is higher than the posted rate. That's only possible, of course, if the saver leaves the interest already earned on deposit in the account so that interest will be paid on interest.

There's even more to it than that. The banks have considerable discretion in determining the way they will pay interest. How often will they calculate the interest on the money deposited? That's compounding. How often will they add that interest to the principal so that it can earn additional interest? That's crediting. What sum will be used as the basis for figuring interest, especially when withdrawals and deposits are made at odd moments during the life of the account? That's computing.

If a bank wants to boost the posted interest rate as far as possible, it will use its discretion on the three Cs in the most liberal way. But if it wants to seem to be offering a lot more than it does, it can reduce the effective yield considerably by a narrow interpretation of these bases for calculation. On longer-term deposits, these factors are far more explicit than in passbook savings accounts, the type most frequently held.

Compounding: Interest on Interest

When the bank calculates interest, adds it to principal, and then calculates interest on the new amount, that's called compounding. Banks compound interest more frequently these days than a few years ago, because they want savers to believe that their funds are earning as much interest as possible.

Yet the mere speeding up of compounding is misleading. For one thing, the differences in actual interest received are small when compounding is accelerated beyond the quarterly period—once every three months. Look at the interest on $1,000 at 5 percent annual interest, when the interest is compounded:

Continuously	$51.27
Daily	$51.27
Monthly	$51.16
Quarterly	$50.95
Semiannually	$50.63
Annually	$50.00

Next to advertising in connection with interest rates, banks pay most attention to the frequency of compounding. Daily compounding or even continuous compounding sound most impressive. How do they work?

The daily rate is determined by dividing the annual interest rate by the number of days in the year. Banks may use either a 360-day year or the actual year of 365 or 366 days. In 360-day years, each month is considered to have 30 days and each quarter 90 days. Using a 365-day year, the number of days in each quarter varies—90, 91, 92, 93. As a result, even with quarterly compounding on a 365-day account, the amount of interest paid for the fourth quarter is likely to be more than the amount paid for the first quarter of the following year. That may seem odd, if you think that interest should be increasing each quarter when all funds are left on deposit.

In an effort to increase effective yields, some savings institutions use a combination of the 360-day and 365-day years. Obviously the daily interest rate for a 360-day year is slightly higher than for a 365-day year (at 5 percent, it's .0001389, as compared with .0001370). Some banks pay the 360-day rate for 365 days. That's why banks can claim an effective yield of 7.9 percent on an annual rate of 7.5 percent. Without this unusual rate mixture, the yield would be only 7.79 percent.

While continuous compounding sounds extremely impressive, for any practical purpose it is essentially a mathematical exercise that yields the same result as daily compounding. At 5 percent on $1 million left in the bank for a year, the difference between continuous and daily compounding would be $4.

According to a 1973 survey by the American Bankers Association, most commercial banks compounded interest quarterly or daily. Generally, it's the smaller banks that compound less frequently. The rate of compounding has been stepped up over the years as competition for savings increased. As money gets easier, savers should be careful to watch whether banks slip back on compounding. Read the fine print in their ads.

All the advertising about compounding and, indeed, all calculations about differing interest payments depending on frequency of compounding mean little if you don't know the rules covering crediting interest to the account.

Crediting: The Money's Yours, or Is It?

You will learn a lot more about the interest you can receive from the frequency of crediting than from how often interest is compounded. For example, a few commercial banks compound and credit daily. But one major bank says it compounds interest daily and pays (another word for credits) it quarterly. Another compounds daily, but credits annually. If you left your money in any of these banks for the full year, you would get the same interest. But if you withdrew funds before the end of a crediting period —in the last case, a full year—you would lose all interest. (Besides crediting rules, you probably need to make sure that a minimum balance remains until the end of the quarter even at banks that compound and credit daily.)

The most recent ABA survey indicated that 93 percent of commercial banks credit interest twice or four times a year. The small banks tend to credit less often than their big brothers. Because only 5 percent of commercial banks credit interest as frequently as monthly or daily, the implication that more frequent compounding means more interest may be misleading. That depends on how long you leave your money in the bank and on crediting rules.

Obviously, the more frequent the crediting, the better the yield for savers. But the chances are great that you won't find banks crediting interest more frequently than four times a year. Even on day-of-deposit–day-of-withdrawal accounts, interest probably isn't credited more than quarterly, although it may be compounded for every day you have it on deposit. If, say, you withdraw funds on October 31, interest on those funds for the calendar quarter beginning October 1 won't actually be paid to you until December 31, and then only if you have maintained a minimum balance until the end of the year.

Mike Pellegrino, who left no balance when he cashed in his accounts, lost interest because the accounts were closed before the end of the calendar quarter. The fact that he had left the money for exactly four years was of no importance. Because the accounts began and ended on different dates relative to the end of the quarter, the lost interest varied, thus accounting for the different amounts he received on each account.

Computing: LIFO, FIFO, and Grace

Almost every saver has heard of compounding. A few are familiar with crediting. But almost none has ever paid any attention to computation. Yet computing methods can have a far greater impact on the interest received than either of the other two elements.

Commercial banks, in particular, use a wide variety of methods for determining the balance on which interest will be calculated. The American Bankers Association has surveyed its members over the years and has found literally scores of variations. Most related to savings accounts in which withdrawals and deposits can be and are made at any time. Many people may not realize that when they withdraw money, the bank will determine which of the dollars in the account—those deposited a long time ago or those deposited recently—are actually paid. That determination can affect how much interest you receive.

Professor L. D. Morse of Kansas State University and Ms. Jackie Pinson, one of his former graduate students, have done most of the detailed research that reveals just how wide the variations can be among banks. They have found six basic computing methods used by most banks:

Low balance: Interest is calculated only on the lowest balance in the account at any time during the crediting period.

Day of deposit to day of withdrawal: Interest is calculated on all funds in the account for as long as they are on deposit.

Day of deposit to end of crediting period: Interest is calculated only on funds left in the account until the end of the period.

FIFO, beginning balance: Interest is calculated on funds in the account after withdrawals are deducted from money in the account for the longest period of time, beginning with money in the account at the beginning of the crediting period. FIFO means "first in, first out."

FIFO, first deposit: Same as FIFO above, except that withdrawals are deducted from the earliest deposits during the crediting period.

LIFO: Same as FIFO above, except that withdrawals are deducted from the most recent deposits and then other deposits in reverse chronological order. LIFO means "last in, first out."

The 1973 ABA survey reflected the growing popularity of the day-of-deposit–day-of-withdrawal method. It was the most frequently used method, favored by 46 percent of the commercial banks. This method is most advantageous to consumers.

The low-balance method was still favored by 30 percent of the commercial banks. It is most advantageous for them because they do not have to pay any interest on funds left in the account in excess of the minimum during the compounding period.

The FIFO approach was used by 16 percent of the banks. This method, too, is more advantageous to the bank than to the customer. A distant fourth was LIFO, which is fairer to the customer, whose "old" money is left untouched until recent deposits are withdrawn. The other methods trailed in popularity.

Grace Days

Although the method of determining the balance for the purpose of calculating interest is in itself quite significant, other factors come into play in the calculation process. One of these is "grace days."

On certain types of accounts, banks will allow grace days to depositors. If, for example, a deposit is made to a passbook account on the tenth of the month, interest will be calculated from the first of that month. Because interest is actually paid on deposits that were not in the bank, the interest rate is, in effect, increased. The ABA survey found that four-fifths of commercial banks allow grace days, normally up to ten days, although some allow fewer days. Generally, the grace period covers the first days of the month at the beginning of the quarter. This feature will be of importance mainly to people who want to make deposits at quarterly intervals, but who do not receive the funds they want to save until the first day of the quarter. Some day-of-deposit–day-of-withdrawal accounts now include grace-day features for deposits at the beginning of a quarter (and for withdrawals at the end). That's a good deal.

Savings accounts may also include a grace period for withdrawals. A saver may be allowed to withdraw funds before the end of the period and yet be paid interest as though the funds had remained in the bank until the last day of the period. Only about a quarter of the banks offer this feature, and the normal grace period is three days.

Many consumers would find that grace days for withdrawal are far more useful than grace days for deposits. Frequently a tax or other bill is due at the first of the month and a savings account will have to be tapped in order to meet the expense. It's far better to be able to withdraw the money in time to pay the bill without losing any interest than either to lose interest or be late in making the payment.

Grace days can be used by what might be called "money jugglers" to increase the effective yield on savings. Most of the juggling these people do, often based on shifting money between banks and using uncollected funds—balances against which they have written checks that have not yet cleared—is too risky for most people. The way they use grace days will illustrate the method.

On January 2, Mr. Jones deposits $1,000 at a thrift paying 5 percent in a day-of-deposit–day-of-withdrawal account with interest compounded daily and paid quarterly. This account, number 1, also gives ten grace days at the beginning of each quarter and three at the end. On January 10, he withdraws the $1,000 from account 1 and deposits it in an identical account, No. 2. By the end of March, the $1,000 will have earned $12.50 from account 2 and $1.09 from account 1. On March 29, taking advantage of the withdrawal grace days, Jonesy the Juggler takes $1,012.50 from account 2 and puts it back into account 1, where it will remain until April 10. Then the process is repeated at the beginning of each quarter.

By redepositing interest and juggling his funds, Jones obtains an annual interest rate of 5.85 percent. If he had merely left his funds in account 1 for the entire year, he would have had an effective rate of 5.13 percent. In short, the juggling put Jones some $7.20 ahead for the year. He worked for that money.

About one-fouth of the commercial banks may penalize their depositors for making too many withdrawals. Two withdrawals every three months may be all you get. If you take money out of your savings account too often—the amount doesn't matter—the bank may slap on a fee. Most charge from 50 cents to $1 for each withdrawal beyond a certain number during a specified period. This fee is charged no matter what the remaining balance. A smaller number of banks link the fee to the balance. This kind of activity fee is obviously designed to discourage withdrawals, which will make it difficult for the bank to plan on how much money it has available to lend, and to prevent savers from using their accounts like checking accounts.

Using five of the computation methods listed above plus the four other variables (compounding, crediting, grace days, withdrawal penalties), Ms. Pinson constructed forty different model savings accounts using exactly the same data. In the six months for which she kept her hypothetical accounts open, they never had a balance exceeding $4,000. The interest yield for the forty accounts ranged from $29.95 to $79.13. That amounts to a difference of 264 percent between the highest and the lowest. She also checked on seven banks and found the range between $36.67 and $58.72—a 60-percent difference. Later checking indicates that Ms. Pinson's survey findings continue to be borne out. Those banks using FIFO practices and semiannual compounding and crediting bring up the rear in interest payments. Banks with quarterly compounding and crediting on a day-of-deposit–day-of-withdrawal basis provide substantially better yields. The best deal, although virtually impossible to find, would be daily compounding and crediting on a day-of-deposit–day-of-withdrawal basis.

Other factors affecting the return on savings are penalties for closing an account early, minimum-balance requirements, and charges for "inactive accounts."

You may have to pay from 50 cents to $5 if you close out an account before a fixed period has elapsed—usually a month or a quarter, but in one case in California, a year.

Some banks won't pay you a cent of interest if you don't leave a minimum balance in the account throughout a quarter. The lowest required balance in any bank is $1. But in some banks you can have $99 in your account and receive no interest because the minimum is $100. Of course, the bank is receiving interest on every cent in the account.

A California study by San Francisco Consumer Action found that if there are no deposits or withdrawals for five years, the account is considered inactive. Then, the banks begin charging "maintenance" fees, which can go as high as $2 a month. Nationally, these charges go as high as $4 a month. Consumers Union says that commercial banks levy these fees more often than savings and loans. Almost two hundred years ago, Benjamin Franklin left $5 to the city of Boston on the condition that the funds be left on deposit for two centuries. Had the "inactivity" rule been in effect, that account would have been wiped out. Instead, Boston will receive some $14 million as a result of the bequest.

It's Not What You See, It's What You Get

Savings institutions, like other commercial enterprises, seek to make their product appear as attractive as possible through their advertising. In general, that means stressing the annual yield more than the actual annual interest rate, even though that yield rate is based on the depositor's leaving all interest on deposit and interest being paid on that interest. An officer of a New England savings bank responded to our survey. "We have not advertised yields. The rate is always constant, the yield is not. It depends on whether or not withdrawals are made on the account, and we feel that we will advertise only those things that are constant, in this case the rate." That view is exceptional. Following are the maximum yield rates, using the 365/360-day year and with interest left in the account.

	Rate Ceiling	*Annual Yield*
Passbook accounts	5.25%	5.47%
Time deposits maturing in:		
90 days to 1 year	5.75%	6.00%
1 to 2½ years	6.50%	6.81%
2½ years or more *	6.75%	7.08%
4 to 6 years	7.50%	7.90%
6 years or more *	7.75%	8.17%

* Generally, no more than 7 years.

Actually, most of the added interest results from leaving interest in the thrift rather than from the 365/360-day compounding method.

As we have seen, the actual yield depends not only on the funds left on deposit, but also on the three Cs. As a result, Professor Morse developed a "truth-in-savings" bill, which then Senator Vance Hartke introduced in Congress. This bill would have required a considerable amount of information to be given to each potential depositor, including the annual percentage rate, the minimum length of time funds must remain on deposit, the annual percentage yield, the percentage rate for each crediting period and the method used to determine the balance for computation of interest, the number of times each year that interest is compounded, the dates on which earnings are credited, any "costs" and their method of computation and limits on them, and any other conditions that alter the rate of earnings payable.

The Federal Reserve and the FDIC have issued rules requiring that yields not be given greater prominence in ads than actual interest rates and that withdrawal penalties be stated.

Banks were asked by the Fed to comment on the desirability of establishing a single method of computation. The commercial banks opposed any single method.

The American Bankers Association said that commercial banks can partially close the rate differentials, established by regulation, between commercial banks and other savings institutions by using liberal computing methods. Savings and loans argued against a single method of computation on the grounds that it would reduce competition among banks by narrowing the variety of choices available to consumers. While the mutual savings banks made similar arguments, they indicate willingness to accept day-of-deposit-day-of-withdrawal or daily compounding with monthly crediting (although they do not indicate the computing method for deposits of less than a month). Finally, the credit unions would have accepted a uniform computation method that required funds to be left until the end of a crediting period, using day-of-deposit-day-of-withdrawal for computation. But they would have preferred a variety of computation rules in order to permit the widest competition among institutions.

Bankers say they are willing to see greater disclosure of information about savings accounts. "Full disclosure will result in a more informed savings public able to understand and compare interest rates, yields to maturity, computation of interest, and other terms which will result in better service and increased competition between financial institutions for savings deposits," says James D. Farley, executive vice-president of Citibank. What "increased competition" generally means is that all banks in a market area have to offer the same return, generally at the highest level permitted. But as long as the consumer remains in the dark about interest calculation, they may only seem to be offering the same interest.

The Bank of America, the nation's largest, says that it favors full disclosure, but maintains that it would be impractical to include all details of interest calculation in advertising. Instead, it suggests that the information should be made available when the account is opened. At the moment, almost no bank provides written information on interest calculation to new-account savers. Very often the depositor doesn't have the opportunity to read all the literature he's been given until after the account has been opened. If the Bank of America is correct, then the regulators would have to prescribe an explanatory text and require that a person opening a new account sign, indicating that he or she has read it. Incidentally, the Bank of America went further than other commercial banks in favoring a single calculating method—day-of-deposit-day-of-withdrawal for a 365-day year. That's the most beneficial for consumers.

Without full disclosure, bank advertising leaves a lot of questions unanswered and can easily mislead the customer. It's all intended to bring in customers, and obviously, some banks believe that full disclosure will undermine the attractiveness of the accounts they offer.

Some banks don't just sell their accounts, they use merchandise as a "come-on." Gifts are offered to people opening a new account or adding a deposit to their present account. Gifts don't indicate much about the terms of the bank's accounts themselves and may very well represent interest in another form. For example, a bank might use semiannual crediting rather than quarterly crediting, with the difference in interest going toward the purchase of the gift. And even if the gift does not detract from interest, the saver should be careful not to lose any interest in the process of transferring funds from an old account to a new one. Finally, the bank revenues that go to gifts may be taken away from another bank service that you desire.

One woman saw that a local bank was offering a "free" tree for each new $1,000 account. She promptly put no less than $17,000 in the bank, hoping for enough trees to landscape her yard. She was crestfallen when she learned that she would get only one tree because she had opened only one account. Presumably, her backyard is still barren. Still another incentive to putting at least $5,000 in a thrift and leaving it there is a free private club for big savers. First organized by State Mutual Savings and Loan in Los Angeles, the clubs have spread East. It took eight years for them to make it to New York, where First Federal opened a club in 1975. With all their comforts and facilities, the one hundred or so clubs discourage depositors from making withdrawals below the minimum.

A Penny Saved . . .

Savings are a lot more complex than they appear, but the consumer who takes the time to figure out the best deal is almost certain to come out ahead.

Here are some things to watch for:

1. The bigger the savings account balance, the more important it is to maximize interest. No matter how small the fractional difference, it is a difference, and its impact grows enormously as the amount of money involved grows. Even if your account is small relative to others, it's probably of major importance to you. So, if you have a savings account, presumably you want to get everything out of it the law allows. Don't just look at the dollar amount involved; calculate how much better you do on interest on one account as compared with another.

2. Remember that commercial banks, while more convenient, cannot pay as high interest as savings institutions. Unless funds are going to be needed regularly and on short notice, and you want to avoid trips to both a commercial bank and a thrift, it may be worth the additional effort to put funds into a savings and loan or a savings bank. Of course, if you have no checking account, use a thrift for savings. Where you choose to save your money may be related to where you will borrow money later. It is often worthwhile to have an account at the institution where you will later apply for a mortgage. In times of tight money, customers with whom the bank is familiar often get some preference. The outlook is for thrifts to be authorized to offer checking accounts. Then, go to the bank that offers the best interest.

3. An almost iron law of banking says that the larger the institution, the more likely it will be to pay the maximum interest the law will allow. Large banks are usually located in the most competitive markets and they can only succeed by offering the most. In addition, they have the computer capacity to handle the difficult calculations often required on more sophisticated accounts. Finally, they are located in markets that allow them to relend their funds—on de-

posit—for everything from mortgages to business loans—at the best return available. But they do not offer the same kind of customer service as smaller banks, mainly because they have so many customers that they don't know their own account holders.

Just because the big banks generally pay at a higher rate than the small ones does not mean that you should accept this as automatically true. About a quarter of commercial banks pay below the ceilings, and they include Citibank and the Bank of America as well as several others in California. A higher percentage of both savings and loans and savings banks pay at the ceiling rate than commercial banks, but the size rule remains valid for them as well.

4. The part of the country where you have your savings account can make a difference. Not only do variations exist for the prevailing interest rate, but also for such matters as frequency of compounding and crediting and the basis for computation.

For commercial banks—the great majority of all banks—the American Bankers Association has found that the customer gets the best deal in the Pacific states and New England and the worst in the North Central part of the country. Although the Mid-Atlantic region does not rate particularly high, it's likely that the New York City area is as favorable as the Pacific region—at least among big banks.

It's wise for the saver to consider opening an account where the terms are best. There may be no need to keep a seldom-used account right in town. Virtually all the banks that are likely to offer attractive terms also offer cost-free bank-by-mail arrangements. Obviously, if you live on a farm in the Midwest, you may not be familiar with the names of major California banks. Your library can help with the name and address and then you can write away for information.

5. Analyze your future needs before you select an account. If you can set a portion of your fund aside for a relatively long period, you can consider a higher-interest account. It may be better to put funds in a high-interest account, even if there's a risk that the penalty will have to be paid if you have to withdraw a small portion of the

savings prematurely, than to place the entire amount in a low-interest account.

For example, if you put $2,000 in a 7.5-percent four-year account and decided to withdraw $500 at the end of two years, the net interest paid for the two-year period, even taking into account the penalty of the amount withdrawn, would be $295.34. If you simply put that same $2,000 in a standard 5.25-percent account on which there would be no penalty for the $500 withdrawal, the interest paid at the end of two years would be $224.78. As a result, you would gain $70.56 by placing your money in a higher-rate account, even if you expected to withdraw a part of it.

For those who may have to withdraw their savings at any time, the best account may well be a day-of-deposit–day-of-withdrawal account. If you can leave your money at least until the end of a calendar quarter, and if you can qualify, the best deal is probably a credit union. The interest rate it pays exceeds the rate paid in so-called grace-day accounts, which are equivalent at the bank. In addition, credit unions offer extremely favorable lending rates to their own depositors.

To be able to profit from the choice of an account, it is essential to plan savings carefully.

6. Check to see if the savings institution is insured (it almost certainly is), but don't place too much stock in what account insurance can do. Of course, it will protect up to $40,000 per account in case of bank failure. That means that Federal and state examiners are interested in determining if the bank is managed properly. But they do not check the math on your account or determine if your interest has been calculated properly. That's up to you, and you can get some help at the bank on request.

7. Don't be overly impressed by how often interest is compounded unless you know how often it is credited or paid into the account. The best deal is day-of-deposit–day-of-withdrawal with daily compounding and crediting.

8. Check into how interest is computed. The computation method may lead you to try another bank. If not, it will help you to determine the effect of withdrawals on the in-

terest you are paid. Occasionally delaying a withdrawal a couple of days can make a difference. For example, if interest is calculated on the basis of the lowest balance in the account during a quarter, it would be unwise to make a withdrawal just a week before the quarter ends. All of the interest on those funds withdrawn would be lost. That's also why it's a good idea to know about grace days. It may take several tries before you find a bank officer who can answer all your questions. Aim for as low a minimum balance as possible.

9. Unless you are terribly weak-willed, you should stay away from Christmas Clubs and the like. You can accomplish the same purpose with a savings account. In a club you can lose all the interest on all of the money in the club simply by missing a single deposit. And some banks offer little or no interest at all.

10. If you are eligible, consider establishing a Keogh Plan or an IRA. The money you deposit and the interest that money earns will not be taxable. It will be taxed only when withdrawn for retirement purposes. Because your income is likely to be lower then, you'll pay less in taxes. If you are saving for your retirement, these plans may be the most beneficial.

11. Ask questions. Bank disclosure, even the best, is not likely to give all of the information you need to get the best deal. The bank is in business to make a profit, and the customer is responsible, as in all transactions, for looking out for himself. Do not assume that, just because the bank looks official and is subject to government supervision, bank officers will volunteer information that will increase your funds and decrease the bank's profits.

Gilbert and Sullivan wrote: "Things are seldom what they seem. / Skim milk masquerades as cream." That's still true, and it's up to you to skim the cream for yourself.

4 The Legal Loan Shark

Fortunately for most people, the only contact they have with a loan shark is in the movies. Few of us have to do with people who lend us money without any fixed date for repayment and keep piling on exorbitant interest charges all the time the loan is outstanding.

Or do we? Loan sharks actually do flourish. But as the saying goes, "for those who qualify," there is a better way. For a mere 18 percent you can borrow money from the bank. You can borrow a couple of thousand dollars from a bank without even setting foot on the premises. You can take just about as long as you want to repay the loan. All you have to pay is 18 percent annual interest, and the bank will probably find a way to calculate the interest that can drive the effective rate up another three points. In addition, the bank probably won't let you borrow the money at any lower rate, so if you want consumer credit and can't put up collateral, you have to borrow at these prices. At least you probably meet a better class of people at the bank than at the loan shark's.

What made free-and-easy mass credit possible, more than anything else, was the development of the plastic chip, the stuff credit cards are made of. In 1951, the ill-fated Franklin National Bank issued the first bank credit card, the forerunner of today's mammoth BankAmericard (which is gradually being renamed Visa) and Master Charge cards. Even in the early days, Franklin National and others quickly learned that operating a credit-card system could be costly and cumbersome. So the new form of credit sputtered along and was joined in 1955 by a check-credit plan, designed to make it possible to extend credit to bank customers without all the complications of the credit card.

Check-credit allows the account holder to write checks for amounts exceeding his or her balance, thus automatically borrowing money from the bank. Begun by Boston's First National Bank, check-credit began to attract other banks that wanted to keep out of the credit-card business. But banks generally stayed away from both of the new forms of credit until ten years later, when they realized that they could bring about a credit explosion and sharply increase their loan portfolio by pushing the plans.

By the end of 1972, the bank credit card and check-credit had swept the country. Credit cards were available in every state, while check-credit, far less popular, was concentrated in the Northeast and Far West. Neither appeared to be limited to those states that permit the highest interest rates to be charged. Between 1968 and 1977, the amount of credit outstanding in bank credit-card schemes had increased some 841 percent. Check-credit outstanding in balances had jumped by 380 percent. By way of comparison, the growth in credit in installment retail charge accounts was only 59 percent during the same period.

At the end of 1972, the last year for which complete figures have been published, some 8,574 banks participated in credit-card plans, with 1,621 operating check-credit plans. Of course, there was some duplication. The amounts of money involved were even more striking. By the beginning of 1977, some $11 billion in credit had been extended through bank credit cards and $3 billion through check-credit. Together, they represented more than 16.5 percent of all consumer installment credit extended by banks. As recently as 1967, they had amounted to only 3.8 percent of all consumer installment credit.

Pick a Card

The bank credit card is, above all, a way of charging retail purchases. The customer gets a monthly bill including purchases made in the last 30 to 60 days. If the bill is paid promptly, there is no interest charge. In effect, the customer has borrowed money from the bank for about a 30-day period without paying any interest. The bank receives anywhere from 1 to 10 percent of the amount of the sale from the merchant.

Credit comes into play when the customer does not immediately pay all of the amount owed. At that point, the bank begins to levy a finance charge and may also exact a number of other fees. Some two-thirds of all people who use bank credit cards take advantage of the credit made available and, in effect, borrow money from the bank. In addition to the interest, the bank still receives the merchant discount fee.

Subject to the limits in state law, the bank can set the interest rate far higher than it charges for regular consumer loans. In most cases, the interest rate is 1.5 percent each month on the average daily unpaid balance, which amounts to an annual interest rate of 18 percent.

Maximum Credit-Card Rates

18%	APR * (1.5% per month)	All states, except:
15%	(1.25% per month)	Pennsylvania
12%	(1% per month)	Connecticut, Hawaii, Kentucky, Minnesota, Washington
10%	(.83% per month)	Arkansas, Florida, Oregon, South Dakota

* APR = Annual Percentage Rate, or simple interest. See Chapter 5.

The customer is usually required to pay only a minimum. For example, if the balance is $10 to $200, a customer might be required to pay at least $10, but no more than 5 percent of the balance if it exceeds $200.

This kind of credit is tempting. You can take as long as

you want, subject only to the small monthly minimum for purchases you make, a feature designed to encourage the increase of consumer purchasing. In addition, you may be able to borrow automatically from a cash-reserve feature of the credit card. In some cases, this may serve as a back-up if you overdraw your checking account balance. It may be linked to banking-by-phone services to protect you from giving oral instructions to withdraw money from your account in excess of your current balance.

But this credit is expensive. In effect, you pay a premium for being able to borrow money whenever you wish and in small amounts. The bank is certainly in no hurry for you to repay this credit, so long as you keep your monthly checks coming, because it makes money on the interest charged on your outstanding balance.

Some people use bank credit cards as a convenience, and you are certainly under no obligation to allow a balance to continue from month to month. However, if you regularly pay the full balance within three weeks or a month, the bank receives no interest from you. Some banks claim that, in this case, they actually lose money on your account, despite the payments they receive from the stores where you have used your card. They may levy a monthly service charge, when you don't borrow money. If you feel that such a charge is unfair, you should certainly let the bank know. The service charge is still fairly experimental, and banks are sensitive to consumer complaints. You can also expect to find competition among banks in making this charge, so you may find it wise to shop around. In addition, let merchants who accept the card know how you feel. They are voting members of credit card associations, the groups which set the terms.

The bank credit card is what is called revolving or open-end credit. That means there is no fixed deadline to have repaid all that you have borrowed. You may have a virtually permanent debt, which means that the bank is continuing to collect interest. Indeed, most monthly credit-card statements have emphasized the minimum payment due rather than the total balance as a way of encouraging customers to borrow money. That is plainly against the law. Obviously, the bank hopes you will be hooked on credit and keep charging and then paying only the minimum required. You may find yourself a lot deeper in debt than you thought. For example, *Changing Times* magazine determined just how long it would take a consumer to pay off $600 in purchases with no additional purchases made later. Using an interest rate of 1 percent when the balance was above $500 and 1.5 percent when it fell below that level, and limiting payments to the required minimum—10 percent of the balance with a floor of $10—the consumer would be in debt for 41 months. The total amount of interest paid would have been $116.15, or some 19.4 percent of the basic purchase price. Had the consumer made payments faster than was required, the interest rate would have been reduced.

The bank can get even more interest if it chooses certain methods for calculating the balance on which the interest will be levied. Most banks use the average-daily-balance method. They calculate the balance outstanding on each day of the month, add them, and divide by the number of days in the billing month. That average daily balance is then multiplied by the daily interest rate. This method includes all of the month's purchases and payments. A modified version of this approach excludes the current month's purchases. This way, an early payment can actually lower the finance cost by covering the cost of recent purchases before they appear.

Retailers have usually favored the previous-balance method, where finance charges are based on what you owed at the end of the past billing month. It takes no account of current payments and purchases.

The adjusted-balance method is best for the consumer. Payments made during the month are deducted from last month's balance and then current purchases are entered.

Another method is the ending balance. Finance charges are levied on the basis of the current month's balance, which reflects all payments and purchases made during the month. The true actuarial average daily balance amounts to the same thing as the ending-balance method, except that even if all purchases are fully paid for by the end of the month, the consumer must pay finance charges on the purchase amounts for any period they were outstanding. It is rarely used.

The difference in cost among these methods can be substantial. Professor E. Ray McAlister of North Texas University found that the average outstanding balance in one retail chain was $91.90 and calculated what the finance charges would be at the same interest rate but applying the various methods:

$1.47	true actuarial—rarely used
$1.41	ending balance
$1.24	previous balance (retailers) and average daily balance (banks)
$1.18	modified average daily balance
$1.09	adjusted balance

That is a differential of 14 percent between the method most beneficial to consumers and the one most often used by banks.

Credit cards may either bear the bank's own imprint or they may be part of a national system. At the outset, banks frequently opted for their own card, but in recent years, two national arrangements, BankAmericard and Master Charge, have come to predominate. Their chief advantage is an interbank clearing system that allows the customer to use the card anywhere in the country. Obviously, the local cards are only accepted by local merchants. By the end of 1972, almost 95 percent of all bank-credit-card systems were affiliated either with National BankAmericard, Inc., or with Interbank Card Association (of which Master Charge is a part). The outfits do not themselves issue the cards or provide credit; they are clearinghouses among banks, known as interchanges, for transferring charges made in one part of the country to the purchaser's bank in another part of the country. They also centralize information on whether the customer pays his credit-card bills promptly. In 1972, almost one-third of credit-card purchasers benefited from the national interchange service.

Banks may be either principals or agents. About one-fifth of them act as principals, which means that all of the credit drawn by their customers comes from that bank alone. The principal bank may in turn line up other banks as agents. Some are "simple agents," meaning that the principal bank continues to be the source of all the credit, while the agent processes the paperwork and, of course, promotes the use of the card. If the bank is a "participating agent," it extends some of the credit, usually no more than 50 percent. Obviously, only principal and participating-agent banks can use the "offset," a procedure that allows them to recover money a customer owes on the credit-card account by dipping into that customer's other accounts. Of the 8,574 banks with credit-card systems, some 1,631 were either principals or participating agents.

Because each credit card is, in fact, issued by a bank, each card holder must establish a relationship with a specific bank, not with BankAmericard or Master Charge.

The Card Game

When you want a bank credit card, you must apply for it. Although that may seem obvious, when these cards were first launched, they were sent by the hundreds of thousands to people who seemed to have the right profile to become frequent card users. The result was a fiasco. Cards were stolen from the mails, used, and then the bills began to arrive at the addresses of many persons who, in fact, had never used the cards. In Chicago, when mass mailings were made in 1966, children received cards and many people received more than one card from more than one bank. The frauds that resulted cost the banks as much as $6 million. While, obviously, mass mailings were the best way of lining up a large number of card holders, the abuses were serious and eventually unsolicited mailings of credit cards were outlawed.

Even so, it is still possible to obtain a credit card without seeking it. When, for example, Chemical Bank installed automatic cash-dispensing machines, customers could either apply for a ChemBank Card or a Special Master Charge Card that could be used to activate the machine. But in one brochure, "NOW Cash Machine Membership FREE thru Nov. 1975," the application form provided no option to ask for the ChemBank Card without the Master Charge feature. And when a customer went to the bank and asked for an application for use of the automatic machine, he found himself filling out an application for Master Charge. Had he not questioned all of the personal finance data that seemed to be required just to be able to use the cash machine, he would not have been informed that he was, in fact, applying for a credit card. The Federal Reserve, which enforces the Truth-in-Lending Act, has been notably benevolent toward the widest propagation of credit cards and has done nothing to block this kind of unsolicited issuance of cards.

But if you fill out an application willingly, be prepared to provide the same kind of information that would be required if you were seeking a consumer loan. While you are expected to reveal a good deal of personal information about your financial condition, the bank may be a good deal less willing to explain the details of the agreement you are making. For example, Chase Manhattan devoted space on its application folder to an offer for place mats provided as a premium to applicants, but said nothing about the interest rates charged on credit, conditions under which customers will be held liable for repayment, and the bank's use of offset. Chemical Bank's Master Charge offered no place mats and no details on the credit agreement other than to state that the card holder will be "subject to the terms and conditions of the Chemical Bank Master Charge Agreement, a New York Retail Installment Credit Arrangement." Presumably that statement is designed to give the potential card holder the reassurance that the agreement he is signing, sight unseen, has been approved by an official agency.

You can obtain a copy of the agreement if you ask or manage to pick up the proper brochure. You may be happier not knowing the terms and conditions. Chemical Bank listed a number of reasons for default, including "termination of present employment." It mattered little to Chemical that you got a new job. "In any event," the agreement read "the Unpaid Balance shall be due and payable . . . all without notice or demand." Elsewhere it stated: "Your [the bank's] opinion as to the existence of such failure of performance is conclusive." The bank could then determine the entire balance is due, without being required to inform the card holder. In short, you might innocently change jobs and find the bank claiming you have defaulted. And you have no right, under the contract, to protest that employment was continuous. While the bank may not use this or other provisions of the contract in most cases, it has the right to do so at any time. Another provision of the agreement has the prospective card holder waiving his constitutional right to trial by jury. And it is possible to accept such conditions without even knowing of their existence if you use one of Chemical Bank's brochures that does not include any details of the agreement. You cannot negotiate this contract, and after you've read the fine print, you may not want a credit card. In any case, you should know what you are signing.

You will pick up your card at the bank, which does not want to risk its loss in the mail. You can begin using it immediately. If your first purchase is for, say, $100 at a local store that is signed up with the same bank that issues your card, the store will get credit for that amount less the discount, perhaps $3. So, it will have $97 credited to its account. You may not actually pay the bank for another 45 days, at which time you pay $100. For having lent the store $97 for the 45 days, the bank gets 3 percent interest for the period, which works out to 24 percent on an annual basis.

If the store is affiliated with another bank, its own bank

will skim a fee of about $1.15 for the transaction before passing the sales slip to your bank. Thus, the merchant's bank will lend the merchant $97 for about 2 days and will receive $1.15 or 1.15 percent interest for 2 days, or 210 percent on an annual basis. Your bank will get $1.85 for lending the same amount for 45 days, which works out to almost 15 percent interest at an annual rate. The difference in profit to your bank between a merchant that is affiliated with it and one affiliated with another bank explains why all banks try to sign up as many merchants as possible or else try to encourage you to repay only the minimum required. The bank is in business to lend money, and the more it can lend, the greater its profit.

You will receive a statement monthly, and you may try to check all of the charges included. But you may find that your bank does not include a copy of all the charge slips—called "country-club billing." Instead, the bank may have resorted to descriptive billing, which reduces mailing weight and allows the bank to enclose additional brochures for other services. That saves the bank billing costs, but customers must ask about any charges they don't understand.

Some statements still place the emphasis on the minimum payment due rather than the total new balance. That temptation to borrow money is a violation of the Federal Truth-in-Lending Act.

"Holder-in-Due-Course"

Until now, if a card holder was dissatisfied with a purchase made with a card, he or she was still obliged to pay the monthly bill and then take the matter up with the merchant. In effect, there was no "stop-payment" provision under a credit-card agreement. Then, in October 1974, Congress passed the Fair Credit Billing Act with an effective date one year later. Now, the credit-card issuer, not the card holder, is liable if the merchandise is unsatisfactory. However, this provision applies only to purchases involving more than $50 and made in the card holder's own state or within 100 miles of his or her billing address. Hence, the bank card issuer will not help the person who has made small purchases or mail-order or other transactions a long way from home. But this is a major reversal of the "holder-in-due-course doctrine," which provides that you must pay the bank—which in the due course of events holds your debt—and then take your complaint up with the merchant. You had little chance of gaining satisfaction on the complaint, because the bill had been paid. Now the bank must assume responsibility for having signed up a merchant who does not meet his commitments.

Another problem that a card holder might encounter is a monthly statement that arrives so late that the card holder cannot avoid an interest payment. The new law requires the bank to mail the statement at least 14 days before the due date. The card holder has 60 days to claim a billing error, and the bank must acknowledge such a claim within 30 days. Within an additional 90 days the bank must either correct the error or carry out an investigation and explain why it believes the statement to be correct. Within these time periods, the bank is banned from threatening the card holder's credit rating and from reporting the account as delinquent to any party. Interest is paid on the disputed amount only if the card holder ultimately accepts the bank's explanation. Of course, if he or she is still unhappy, the card holder can take the bank to court.

Yet another feature of the Fair Credit Billing Act bars the use of setoff unless the card holder has expressly authorized use of it at specific intervals. It is also banned whenever the card holder objects because the charge in question is under dispute.

Beware of any statement or contract for a bank credit card that includes a membership fee. Enough banks provide credit cards free of charge that there is no reason to sign up for a plan that involves any membership charges.

In addition to the finance charge—often at the 18-percent annual rate—the statement may reveal other unexpected fees. If the payment of at least the minimum amount due is not made by a date specified on the statement, a late charge may automatically become due. That charge is usually 5 percent of the minimum payment due, with a minimum of 50 cents and a maximum of $5. While these charges may seem small, they are added to the total balance due and become part of the base figure used for computing interest that is due.

Interest charges that have not been paid are themselves added to the unpaid loan balance and, as a result, the next month's interest is charged not only on the outstanding principal but on outstanding interest. Thus, if the amount owed is $100, the interest at 1.5 percent will add $1.50 to the principal. The following month, interest will be levied on $101.50, not the basic $100.

Merchants price their goods to include the service charge they must pay the bank for the right to accept its credit cards. This charge covers the bank's services as bill collector. In 1974, Consumers Union pressed hard to ensure that if you preferred to pay in cash you would not be obliged to pay this hidden fee. Some credit-card agreements with merchants had actually banned them from giving cash customers a price reduction equal to the merchant's discount paid the issuer. The Consumers Union Washington office brought legal action against several credit-card companies and some agreed to inform their affiliated merchants that they could offer a cash discount. Then, in the Fair Credit Billing Act, Congress specifically banned credit-card companies from preventing cash discounts and provided incentives for merchants to "clearly and conspicuously" disclose that they grant such discounts. While such a provision may encourage purchasers to pay in cash rather than use a credit card, it may also discourage merchants who had urged customers to pay in cash instead of using the credit card because the merchant did not want to give up his "merchant's discount." Now he will have to give it up in either case.

Aces and Jokers

The credit card obviously has some real advantages for the consumer. Rather than open a number of charge accounts, all of which require the annoying and possibly embarrassing exposure of your personal financial situation, a single application can lead to a charge account acceptance by many merchants. Not only can a bank credit card replace charge accounts, it can usually be used in place of a number of special-purpose accounts. Many service stations will accept BankAmericard or Master Charge, although far fewer than before the energy crisis. Of course, the oil companies prefer the customers to use their own card: It breeds customer loyalty and it saves the company the payment of the merchant's discount. In addition, airlines, hotels, and restaurants will often accept bank cards as readily as they will the more usual travel and entertainment cards such as American Express, Diner's Club, and Carte Blanche.

Yet another convenience of the bank credit card is the single monthly statement, which enables the consumer to see many if not most monthly purchases at a single glance. This helps in personal budgeting. It usually also means that only one check need be written where it was formerly necessary to write several. That makes for ease and convenience and may even reduce service charges. In fact, if a person can use his bank credit card to cover most of his monthly bills, he may be able to shift to a less expensive type of checking account, based on substantially reduced activity. Finally, the use of bank credit cards usually allows the individual to carry less cash, which may be an important security measure in areas where people fear robberies.

The consumer must weigh such advantages against serious disadvantages. Credit cards can lead individuals to increase their level of purchases beyond what they need, simply because of the relative ease of payment and the notion that the money can be found later. The traditional warnings of an empty wallet or a checkbook that shows a small balance disappear. Whatever the credit-card companies say by way of denial, the fact that the cards are designed to stimulate increased spending is obvious. Merchants would not be willing to give up the discount to the card issuer if they did not believe that the card would attract customers who might make impulse purchases. This is especially obvious when most if not all merchants in a given market area accept credit cards. The issuer must also be counting on increased purchases, which, more than anything else, would stimulate the use of credit.

An even greater danger is that the consumer will go beyond acceptable debt limits into serious overindebtedness and even bankruptcy. As economic conditions worsen, people may find themselves closer to this line sooner than they expected. A look at the charge-off rate, the percentage of accounts that are written off because of failure to pay the balance, is revealing. While, in theory, the longer a credit-card plan is in existence, the lower the charge-off rate as bad risks are eliminated, the overall rate has actually been climbing each year. In 1967, the rate was 1.97 percent; by 1972, it had risen to 2.32 percent. About 15 to 20 percent of the amounts charged off are due to fraud. That means most of the charge-offs occur because account holders simply are unable to pay the bills they have run up and were aware of their inability to pay at the time the charges were incurred. While a 2.32-percent rate among account holders may not seem like much, it represents about one-tenth of the gross revenues that banks take in from the operation of credit-card systems. In short, the percentage of unpaid credit-card bills is relatively high and appears to be growing continually. Indications are that the charge-off rate for more traditional consumer loans is generally lower.

Other disadvantages include the possibility that record keeping may become more difficult rather than less so with the advent of the descriptive statement. Using this statement, the bank merely sends a list of charges made, not actual copies of the charge receipts. Sometimes it's difficult to recognize a specific item from the cryptic reference on the statement. Another potential problem stems from the loss or theft of a card. The card holder's liability is now limited to $50 if another person begins using the card. To avoid that exposure, the card holder must notify the issuer as soon as possible, citing the missing card's number. There is no liability from the moment the issuer is notified. That's why it's a good idea for the card holder to keep a record of his or her account number separate from the card itself.

Give Yourself Some Credit

A woman is at an auction and spots a chest she absolutely must have. Sold, for $300. Then, to her shock, her checkbook reveals that she has only $250 left in her account. No matter, she simply writes a check for the full amount, thus activating a loan from her bank. Aside from the obvious implication that women are likely to spend beyond their means, this commercial is an obvious invitation to impulse buying. Check-credit, the making of loans by use of a bank checking account, is perhaps the most painless form of credit extension possible.

Some of the check-credit plans are check-overdraft accounts, like the one in the commercial. The account holder has previously arranged a maximum line of credit with the bank and can at any time overdraw the checking account without any fear of paying penalties. Instead, a loan is automatically extended and this may reach the total amount of the credit line. A variation on this approach allows the customer to make an on-the-spot loan without its becoming an overdraft. In effect, a separate loan account is then automatically activated, even though a regular check has been used to make the payment. Still another wrinkle on the overdraft account is the check-guarantee card, which informs the merchant that the bank will back a check issued on a specific account. That increases the acceptability of the check. Of course, such cards are now issued to preferred customers who may not have any overdraft arrangement.

Another type of check-credit arrangement provides for the use of special checks that are linked with a checking account especially opened for the line of credit. In other words, every check written on such an account causes a loan to be opened. A check-guarantee card may be used in conjunction with such an account. The special checks used under such a plan are, in effect, cashier's checks, although they are signed by the customer and not the bank. The full credit of the bank stands behind the check.

While a credit-card customer need not have a checking account at the issuing bank, a person using check-credit must open an account. In particular, the overdraft account means that the person must open a demand-deposit account with some of his or her own funds.

Check-credit plans have obvious advantages for the issuing banks as compared with credit cards. There is no need to make special arrangements with merchants to accept the checks. Of course, the merchant's discount is lost, but the bank is more than compensated by the payment of interest by every person who uses the check-credit system. Unlike the credit-card plans, which allow a grace period for repayment without interest, the check-credit schemes involve the immediate activation of a loan on which interest is charged. The bank may designate the use of the check-credit plan for specific groups of customers and design it to fit the needs of each. As a result, the size of the credit line is likely to be a good deal larger than that attached to a credit card. And once somebody has taken the trouble of opening such an account, the activity is likely to be several times higher than for credit-card accounts. All of this makes check-credit plans more attractive to banks than credit cards, and this is especially true for smaller banks that could not hope to operate their own credit-card plan.

By the same token, check-credit is less popular with consumers than is the credit card. The card at least allows the holder the option of not borrowing funds from the bank, and, as indicated earlier, about one-third of card holders avoid borrowing by promptly paying the full outstanding balance. Presumably, check-credit, which absolutely involves debt, is far less attractive, certainly to those who want convenience, not credit.

The cost of money borrowed under a check-credit

scheme is high. In California, for example, the monthly rate is 1.5 percent, which works out to 18 percent annually. That rate is permitted in many other states and, as in California, a transaction fee may also be levied, which, in effect, pushes interest even higher. The banks that begin charging interest immediately stay away from using such fees. But if interest is not levied until a month after the credit line is activated, fees of either 1 or 2 percent or flat charges ranging from $1 to $2 are levied. A $2 fee on a $100 overdraft amounts to interest at an annual rate of 24 percent.

Just as with credit cards, banks use at least two different methods to determine the balance. Some use the average daily balance and charge interest immediately. Others charge a flat fee for the transaction and delay the start of interest payments until sometime after the loan is made. They use the unpaid balance after the delay period. If the loan is repaid quickly, the daily charge is likely to be less costly than the transaction fee associated with the delayed-action accounts. Over a longer period, the interest cost would be higher on the average-balance account than on the unpaid-balance account.

Perhaps the most serious drawback of the overdraft account is the amount of the loan that is created when the account is activated. In some accounts, you incur a debt only in the exact amount of the overdraft. But in many others, banks require that the loan be made in multiples of $50 or $100. Citibank's Checking Plus account has an automatic $100 minimum. So does its Ready Credit, which is the arrangement for an account that is kept separate from the normal checking account. Yet the brochures for these services give no hint of the minimums involved. The brochure does not tell you that you are obliged to borrow at least $100. If, in using Checking Plus, you overdraw by $50, you are charged interest on a full $100. At a normal 12-percent annual rate, that means you are paying at an annual rate of 24 percent on the $50 loan. By contrast, East River Savings is explicit in stating that borrowing need not be made according to fixed multiples. Bank of America tells you there's a $50 multiple. In case of doubt, the customer should assume there is a minimum multiple and ask what it is. In some places the customer can avoid the minimum by filing a specific written request for a loan in the exact amount desired.

Another hidden problem for the account holder may be in the repayment rules. At Citibank, customers run into trouble if they assume that deposits are automatically credited against loans from their Checking Plus accounts. The Nader study of Citibank quotes one customer:

When my daughter got sick a few months ago, I overdrew my Checking Plus account by $100.00 in order to pay the doctor's bill. When I deposited my paycheck in the account, I assumed that the loan was repaid. When my first monthly statement arrived and indicated that I was still paying interest on the loan, I assumed that it was due to a lag between the time I deposited the money and the time the bank gave me credit for repaying the loan. When the next statement still showed the loan had not been repaid, I went into the branch and was told for the first time that Checking Plus loans must be repaid separately from normal deposits in the account. Nobody ever told me anything.

Chase Manhattan, which always includes the terms of the agreement on the back of its applications for Cash Reserve loans, is explicit: "All deposits to the Account when there is any amount owing shall be deemed payments or prepayments of the amount owing until paid in full with interest." In the absence of such a clear statement, the account holder may easily find that loan charges keep mounting while deposits are being made. Occasionally, the only difference between deposits is that a special form must be used for those deposits which are supposed to reduce the loans.

Other drawbacks of overdraft checking are similar to credit-card plans. The offset is almost always used and applies to all property in possession or under control of the bank. That could be construed to include even the contents of a safe-deposit box. In the event of what the bank determines to be a default, the account holder is also liable for a charge of 15 percent of the amount owed to cover the bank's legal expenses. Finally, the bank may charge a

4-percent late fee each time an installment is more than 10 days overdue. The account holder must keep a sharp watch on the bank's monthly statement for due dates and amounts repayable.

A Little Something in Advance

The hybrid of the bank credit card and the check-credit plan is the cash advance. The credit card is used to purchase a product from a merchant, only this time the product is money and the merchant is the bank itself. The card is brought to the bank and a cash advance is applied for. The total amount cannot exceed the line of credit that was made available to you when you opened the credit-card account. In other words, the line of credit can be used either to cover purchases or in the form of cash paid directly to the account holder.

The cash advance is actually nothing more than a small personal loan. But the interest rate is high—18 percent in many places and 12 percent in New York. In California a one-time transaction fee may also be charged, perhaps as high as 4 percent of the loan. A few banks advance cash in multiples, which may mean that you have to borrow more than you want. Interest is not likely to begin on any advance where a transaction fee is levied if the loan is repaid within a month.

Some banks will provide blank checks for use in paying taxes, insurance premiums, doctors, and others who won't accept payment by credit card. But these checks are, in fact, portable cash advances with the same high interest. You automatically borrow money when the check is presented to the bank for payment. This is simply a variation on check-credit.

Another variation on the theme is the plan linking banks and travel and entertainment credit cards—most notably American Express. Such cards, as well as airline, oil company, and retail store cards, have nothing to do with banks. But through a plan like American Express Executive

Credit, a link is forged. American Express, not the bank, lines up and recruits customers. The card is, in the first instance, a normal American Express credit card, accepted by airlines, restaurants, and hotels. In addition, the card provides a minimum of $2,000 in a credit line, provided by the bank, which can be used to pay the monthly Amex bill (over $100), to buy travelers checks, and to take a loan from the bank, in line with its own procedures. In addition, check-cashing privileges, already available under American Express, are expanded. In short, this is just another bank credit card, although it is accepted by those who may not normally accept the bank's own card.

It's in the Cards

The bank credit card and its cousin, the check-credit account, have come to play a major role in the dispensing of consumer credit. For many people who extend their relationship with a commercial bank beyond the simple checking account, the next step will be establishing a credit arrangement through one of these two plans. They are both designed to be so simple for the customer to use that he or she can be led easily from simply having a checking account to opening a more profitable (for the bank) loan relationship. Although banks' accounting tends to underrate the contribution of credit-card loans to profits, they constitute about 1 percent of the assets of commercial banks. Even more important, of course, is that they may lead to more extended credit arrangements between the account holder and the bank.

Because of their ease and convenience and the relative freedom with which they are issued, they are subject to high interest rates. In late 1976, for example, the average rate for credit-card plans operated by banks was 17.05 percent annually, as compared with 13.26 percent for 12-month personal loans at the same banks and 20.86 percent for personal loans from finance companies, which are expected to take on the highest-risk customers. The credit-card rate is just below the highest rates allowed nationally—18 percent. In short, the banks are taking the maximum the law will allow. Like the loan shark, they seem to be immune from competitive pressure.

The growth of the bank credit card and check-credit has been substantially greater than the increase in other forms of credit. In the period between 1968 and 1974, these gains were registered in the amount of credit outstanding:

Bank credit cards	542%
Check-credit	207%
Credit unions	140%
All consumer credit	72%
Bank personal loans	62%
Retail credit	54%
Finance companies	47%

Credit cards and check-credit have grown a lot faster than credit extended by retail outlets, finance companies, and the banks' own personal loan departments. Of course, the banks have consciously tried to divert small borrowers from their loan departments to credit cards.

Many banks have forced the shift away from personal loans by refusing to make installment loans of less than $1,000, or even $2,000. That means the cheapest way to make a personal loan of that amount or less is by using the credit card. It costs the bank more than $40 to process an installment loan, while the credit-card loan may cost only a fifth that much. The average size of an installment loan in a large bank is $1,763, while a credit-card loan in the same bank averages $244. While an installment loan would be less costly to the customer, the bank in effect raises the cost when the customer wants to borrow only a small amount.

Like just about all other forms of installment credit, but with a great deal more flexibility than most, credit-card loans reflect consumer reactions to economic conditions. When inflation was soaring in 1974, people made increased use of card-credit in order to maintain their standard of living. The continued expansion of credit-card use took place even as borrowing for automobile purchases and at the personal loan department, finance companies, and thrifts all declined. Then, in early 1975, recession cut their use as people could no longer look forward to receiving income later that would cover their current expenditures.

Keeping the Shark from the Door

Welcome to the wonderful world of credit. But remember that the bank is in business to lend you money and that it derives its profits from the interest and fees you pay for the use of that money. Once again, it's up to you to protect yourself.

1. A credit card and a check-credit plan are loan programs designed to encourage you to borrow money. Whatever your intentions in beginning one of these programs, the bank's goal is to get you to borrow. Only one-third of those who have bank credit cards refrain from using the credit facilities made available.

2. Get a copy of the rules and regulations governing the account, take them away from the bank and read them, and then return to open the account when you want. This procedure has several advantages: You get a copy of the rules, often difficult to accomplish without persistence; you have the chance to learn about all or most of the charges and penalties; you can compare the terms of plans offered by several banks. Just because two banks offer the same national credit card is no assurance that the terms they use are the same. Since convenience is not of great importance because you will pay your bill by mail, do not feel obliged to open a credit-card account at a bank where you already have checking or savings accounts. In fact, the offset rule should discourage you from putting all of your eggs in one basket.

3. Analyze your own needs and then compare the cost of borrowing by credit card, check-credit, or cash advance. Even in the same bank the charges will vary considerably. If you expect to borrow, jot down the amount and the length

of time you are likely to need the funds and calculate the charges. Of course, if you already have a credit card, but find a check-credit plan more advantageous, you can open one.

4. It is still possible for you to receive an unsolicited credit card. Do not accept it. If you have shopped around and want a card, you need not pay a membership fee. Try to select a plan in which other fees are as minimal as possible. Ask if the statement is merely descriptive or provides copies of charges. If only a descriptive statement is available, protest to the bank. According to the ABA, descriptive statements are still fairly new and issuers are especially sensitive to customer reaction. These statements will be continued if there are few complaints. If the bank refuses to provide copies of charge slips, you should keep sales slips to compare with the statements.

5. It is best to select either BankAmericard (Visa) or Master Charge because of their wide acceptance. Because bank plans differ, you should ask how the balance is calculated and give preference to the system that uses last month's unpaid balance less the current month's payments and credits.

6. Try to use the credit card as a budgeting and payment method. Pay the full amount of the outstanding balance unless you have decided that you wish to borrow money. Then, the credit card may be the preferable method because it allows you to borrow just the amount you want while avoiding some of the fees associated with check-credit.

7. Take advantage of the provisions of the Fair Credit Billing Act that allow you to protest charges appearing on your statement without being harassed. It may also relieve you of liability for payment for certain purchases when the merchandise was unsatisfactory. Also, check state consumer credit codes that may provide additional coverage. You can do this by contacting the state agencies listed in the Appendix.

8. If you use check-credit, use it sparingly. To avoid impulse buying, it is preferable to open a separate account instead of tacking check-credit on in the form of an over-

draft provision. In that way, there is no possibility of inadvertently drawing down part of the credit line.

9. Determine all of the fees and conditions of check-credit and pay special attention to the amount of the loan that is activated. You should only use a plan that allows you to borrow the amount you want. If you borrow frequently, the worst that can happen is that you will find several overdraft notices on your bank statement that make reconciling it a little more difficult. The plan should also make repayment as easy as possible and not permit situations where deposits are not credited against outstanding loans. Finally, the best plan will not begin charging interest immediately, thus allowing time for repayment as with a credit card. In such a case, determine if there is a transaction fee and its amount.

10. When using a cash advance, determine if it is activated in minimum multiple amounts and is subject to transaction fees. Evaluate the relative utility of cash as compared with using a credit card to make specific purchases. You should probably reject such plans as American Express Executive Card that provide almost no advantages that would not be available through other plans. If you already have BankAmericard or Master Charge, both of which permit long-term repayment, the travel and entertainment card linkup to a bank will offer you little more. These card are now so widely accepted that Amex and other such cards may provide you with little more access to merchants, while requiring a stiff annual membership fee.

11. All of these forms of borrowing are what's known as open-end credit. That means the bank wants you to take as long as you want, within few limits, in order to pay back a loan. It's in your interest to cut repayment time as short as possible. If you need to borrow relatively small sums over longer periods, you would probably do better to take an installment loan from the bank or credit union and handle your short-term debts out of those funds. Otherwise the shark may have caught you.

5 We Give You a Lot of Credit

There is one four-letter word that is music to the ears of most bankers. The word is "loan."

Banks are in business to make a profit, and loans produce the largest profits. So, banks make loans of all varieties available to individual customers. Of course, a major part of banking operations is devoted to loans to business, but the consumer, or personal, loan is, nonetheless, the most important link a bank can establish with its individual customers.

Through extensive marketing efforts, banks try to induce people to borrow money. Indeed, the credit-card and check-overdraft account are, in some respects, a painless introduction to bank credit. The customer may move from this do-it-yourself loan on a small scale to a larger loan from the bank. At the other end of the spectrum is perhaps the largest loan that a person will make, a mortgage loan for the purchase of a home. We'll look at mortgages later.

Credit-card borrowing is what is known as an open-end loan because there is no fixed deadline for repayment. Through a revolving account where new charges and new payments may be made every month, there may always be a loan balance. Other consumer loans that a bank may make are called "closed-end," because they are for a fixed term.

Commercial banks provide about 43 percent of all consumer credit directly and a substantial additional amount indirectly. For example, finance companies account for 20 percent of consumer credit, and they draw a large part of their funds from the banks. Other major sources of consumer credit are credit unions, which represent about 13 percent, and merchants, who account for much of what remains. The total amount of money borrowed by consumers at the end of 1975 was $191 billion.

Most often, people make consumer loans in order to purchase an automobile. Other consumer goods purchases, including mobile homes, are almost as frequently cited as the reason for making a loan. The third major area is the personal loan, which may not be associated with any specific major purchase and which may, in fact, be used to consolidate outstanding debts.

Shopping for Interest Rates

Many people believe that they are at the mercy of the banks when it comes to determining how much they will have to pay for the money they want to borrow. In fact, they have a good deal more discretion than they may realize.

At one extreme, of course, is not borrowing money at all, but waiting until enough has been saved. There is no interest cost at all, and the bank or thrift will contribute interest to the amount you deposit to bring you closer to the sum needed. But there may be an "opportunity cost." Perhaps the price of the item you wish to buy is actually increasing due to inflation. By waiting for a few months, you may end up having to pay more than you have saved by not paying interest. In addition, the interest the bank pays you in taxable income, while interest you pay on a loan is deductible from your income for tax purposes. Preaching to people who are prepared to take a loan when they would do better to save is, in any case, likely to fall on deaf ears. The best interest rates are usually available on passbook loans from thrift institutions and on loans from credit unions.

Savings and loans and savings banks will usually lend an amount almost equal to the full balance in the account you have with them. This loan is easy to contract because it does not have to be reviewed by any loan officer or committee, beyond a verification that the account does, indeed, exist. The rate charged is likely to reflect only a relatively small margin of profit for the thrift above what it pays on savings. Consumers Union has found that thrifts usually charge about 2 percent more than they pay in interest.

A thrift will take possession of the passbook as a simple precaution against withdrawal while the loan is outstanding. But the interest earned by the money on deposit will continue to be credited to your account and entered into the passbook. The depositor should be able to withdraw this interest and that part of the principal which is not needed to back the loan. Some thrifts do not allow the depositor to touch the funds in the account throughout the life of the loan. The borrower should talk with the loan officer about this rule and ask to have it waived if it does apply. If the thrift institution is intransigent and there is sufficient time to transfer funds without losing interest, you may want to change to another thrift. In any case, you certainly should not deposit any more money in an account at that thrift so long as you have an outstanding loan. Simply open a new account in another institution.

Commercial banks usually do not offer low-interest passbook loans on their savings accounts. That's one good reason not to open a savings account in a commercial bank.

Credit unions will let their members take loans against the value of their shares on almost the same terms. Again, the chief attraction of such loans is their low interest rate and the ease in obtaining the money.

The rates that credit unions offer on loans that are not secured by deposits may also be quite attractive. The most that Federal credit unions may charge is 12 percent a year, and in 1973, a year of relatively high rates, 76 percent of loans were made at this rate. But some 17 percent were made at a rate of 9 percent or lower. Because credit unions may have a relatively close relationship with their members, they charge about one percentage point less than commercial banks on personal loans. Some credit unions even refund a part of the interest they have collected during the year to borrowers who had loan balances outstanding during that same year. This is a form of profit-sharing and is designed to encourage members to borrow from the credit union rather than elsewhere.

Because credit unions are often sponsored by employers, they may have a unique relationship with them. One disadvantage is that the credit union can obtain a wage assignment from the borrower as a condition of making the loan and then be able to tap his or her wages directly in case of late payment or nonpayment on a loan not secured by deposits.

Next up the ladder of interest rates are loans obtained from banks and credit unions that are secured by assets other than passbook deposits. Often these are stocks and bonds that the borrower does not plan to sell. Just how much the bank will lend depends on the nature of the security offered. Some are traded on securities exchanges and have a price that can be determined easily each day. Others, which are less attractive, are traded over-the-counter and not on any exchange. The least attractive are shares of closely held corporations, whose shares are held by a few people and are not generally traded. Their price can be determined only by what a purchaser is willing to pay for them at the time they are offered. Outside of this scale are government securities, which are very good backing for a loan and will bring almost full value. Depending on the economic situation and the volatility of the market, the bank may offer 60 to 80 percent of a recognized and listed stock, or 40 to 50 percent of an unlisted stock. And if prices fall, the bank may ask for additional collateral. Finally, if you are pledging stock in order to borrow money to buy more stock, the Federal Reserve Board sets limits on just how much can be borrowed.

The cash value of whole-life insurance policies may also be a suitable security for a consumer loan. Of course, the policyholder can borrow directly from the insurance company up to the cash value and is almost certain to pay only a low interest rate. Chances are that the older the policies, the lower that rate will be. In addition, the principal does not actually have to be repaid as long as interest is either paid regularly or added to the loan amount. The chief drawback in borrowing against the insurance policy from the issuing company itself is that in the event of death the payment will be reduced by the amount of the loan outstanding. As an alternative, the cash value of the policy can be pledged as security at the bank, which in no way affects the amount of insurance. Usually, it will be a good idea to have the beneficiary of the policy also agree to the assignment of the cash value to the bank. In the event of default on the loan, the bank will cash in the policy. That not only reduces insurance, it eliminates it. Thus, a great deal of care should be used in borrowing against a life insurance policy.

The next and probably the most likely step is to turn to a commercial bank or a thrift for an unsecured loan. Again, many people believe that all banks charge the same rates, but a bit of shopping around will quickly reveal that this is not the case. There are significant differences even among banks in the same market. And it is likely that you will have to borrow money in your home market; banks seldom lend to individuals who come to them from another market without an apparently sound reason.

Surveys conducted by Consumers Union and the Federal Reserve Board indicate that small commercial banks usually charge about 1 to 1.5 percent less than large banks for consumer loans. However, this generalization may not apply in every market and even in each bank in relation to loans for various purposes.

It is wise to shop around on rates. Do not sign any papers until you have accumulated comparative data from several banks. Each month, the Federal Reserve publishes national averages of rates for five categories of installment credit. Here are the figures for October 1976 expressed in annual percentage rates, which we'll discuss shortly:

New automobiles (36 months)	11.04%
Mobile homes (84 months)	11.63%
Other consumer goods (24 months)	13.03%
Personal loans (12 months)	13.26%
Credit-card plans	17.05%

Of course, these rates change continually, but these figures are useful as an indication of the relationship among rates for various purposes.

It is impossible for the consumer to go to any single source to determine interest information for a specific market. The Federal Reserve figures are based on monthly information provided by some 350 commercial banks throughout the United States. Consumers Union has sued to make this information public, but the Federal Reserve insists that banks would not be willing to provide information if they could not be confident that it would not be released. In March 1975, Consumers Union obtained and published the interest-rate data submitted by 95 banks in 11 major markets.

The Federal Reserve, which asked for an FBI investigation to determine where Consumers Union got their information, points out that such information is available directly from the banks concerned. The conscientious consumer will have to visit each bank to collect information. What the banks resist is a public compilation of interest-rate data that would make comparison shopping possible without actually going from bank to bank.

The data that Consumers Union made public showed major rate differences even within a single market. In the New York City area, a $2,000 personal loan for a year from Chemical Bank Hudson Valley would cost $130, while the same loan would cost only $109.09 at Irving Trust. In Chicago, the gap was $41.27 between Main Bank's low and Northern Trust's high. The biggest gap in a single market occurred in the Dallas–Fort Worth area, with a low of $108.33 at Republic National Bank and a high of $194.68 at First National Bank of Dallas—a difference of $86.35. The widest national disparity was between First National Bank of New Jersey at the low end and Valley National Bank of Glendale, California, at the high end; the difference worked out to $134.98. Valley National was 238 percent more expensive. Incidentally, the Fed's composite national figure worked out to $145.92, higher than any of the New York or Chicago banks.

Obviously, this is the kind of information that local consumer groups or consumer bureaus in state and local government could compile. The net result of full disclosure of rate information will inevitably be lower interest rates because of open competition.

Not only is it worthwhile to shop around among banks to find the lowest interest rate, but the consumer should also be prepared to bargain with the bank over the specific rate. Remember that the rates quoted to the Federal Reserve are merely the most common, not the only rates charged. In fact, a check at Chemical Bank one day in November 1974, the month covered by the Consumers Union survey, revealed a higher interest rate than the one reported. If you argue that you should be charged less than the original amount the bank quotes, you may succeed in bringing the rate down. The loan officer may be impressed by your other accounts in the bank, your income, your past loan record, and the security you offer. Your willingness to shop around at other banks is also bound to make an impression. The loan officer wants to give you the money as long as he or she feels confident that you won't default.

If you ask, you may find advantageous rates for certain customers. For example, one bank cuts the interest on unsecured personal loans of as much as $10,000 by 1.2 percent for those who have $2,000 (or less, depending upon the loan) in a savings account.

Beyond the commercial banks, in the stratosphere of interest rates you will find automobile dealers and, above all, finance companies. The automobile dealer will probably save you a lot of trouble by offering to take care of financing, but you will pay more than if you went directly to the bank yourself. The finance company exists mainly to lend money to people who cannot get money at the bank. It charges a much higher rate of interest to enable those who pay their loans to help subsidize the finance company for those who default. In addition, the finance company has to charge more because it pays more than does the bank for the money it lends.

While thrift institutions write loans that are secured, in many places they are forbidden to make unsecured personal loans. They are banned from doing so because they might make personal loans in preference to mortgage loans, thus defeating one of their major purposes. A strict limit could be placed on the share of the thrift's assets that could be allocated to personal loans. Chances are that the interest rate charged would be lower than at a commercial bank.

Apply Yourself to the Task at Hand

Whether or not you get a loan depends quite a bit on what may seem a subjective judgment of you and your ability to repay. The bank will want to evaluate your character, your job security, your financial condition, your personal qualifications (especially where you live and how long), and your loan history. Inevitably, as part of gathering this information, a loan officer will interview you. The American Institute of Banking teaches new bankers that there are no less than sixteen danger signals to watch for during a loan interview. Among them are:

> The applicant applies at a bank far removed from his home or work.
>
> The applicant resides in a rooming house . . . a slum area . . . or he uses a post-office box as his address.
>
> The applicant is suspected of being a heavy drinker.
>
> The applicant does not have an established place of business . . . operates out of his home or has a telephone answering service.
>
> The individual enjoys diplomatic immunity.

Of course, many of the warning signs are quite legitimate. But some of those cited above make it difficult if not impossible for diplomats, writers and artists, newcomers to town, or some minority group members to obtain a loan. Of course, the personal preferences of the loan officer may enter into the decision, so that's why some people have a haircut before they go to the bank.

The loan officer is trying to keep his record as clear of "deadbeats" as he can. But a loan officer who keeps his record clear of risks may also keep it clear of loans. In the end, the loan officer will have to take some risk and may, in fact, end up urging loans on people who should not take on added debt.

Not only will this evaluation determine if you get the loan, it may also determine the interest rate to be charged. Other determinants of the interest rate are the amount and nature of the loan. Rates can actually change as the loan amount increases. Well-secured loans, where the items being purchased can serve as collateral, will bring the rate down.

You simply won't be able to get certain personal installment loans because they are too small. You will be obliged to borrow by means of a bank credit card or a check-overdraft account. If you are borrowing a small amount—say, less than $500—for a short period—say, six months or less—you will probably do better to borrow in one of these other ways. You thus avoid paying any minimum fee that the bank may charge for making the loan in case the interest paid doesn't cover its costs, and the prepayment penalty that is levied as part of a closed-end loan if you wish to pay off the loan early. Otherwise, the personal loan will be preferable, because the interest rate is almost certain to be lower than the rate on the credit-card loan.

You Have to Be Calculating

Perhaps the most difficult problem in making a loan is figuring out how much interest you have to pay. For a long time, the interest rate most lenders used gave the impression, obviously intended, that interest was a lot lower than it actually was. In an effort to make it easy for borrowers to compare interest rates asked by various lenders and to get a better idea of the real rate they would pay, the Truth-in-Lending Act requires that the loan be quoted at the Annual Percentage Rate (APR). The APR is calculated on the basis of the amount of the loan principal outstanding at the time of each payment. This is then converted to an annual rate of interest. The APR is also called the simple rate of interest, but figuring it out is by no means simple and the consumer cannot ordinarily handle the computations. The lender will provide the dollar amount of interest to be paid, if you ask. That's why the APR must be regarded as an abstract figure, not as the real price tag.

Before the requirement to use the APR, many lenders gave the so-called add-on rate. An add-on of 6 percent meant that it cost $6 to borrow $100 for a year. If payments were made monthly, the total amount to be repaid was $106, or $8.83 per month. That was easy enough for the borrower to calculate. The drawback was that the 6 percent substantially misrepresented the actual interest paid. With each monthly payment, a part of the $100 principal was repaid, so the borrower did not have use of the money for the full year. Yet interest of $6 was calculated as though the $100 were not repaid until the full year had elapsed. Because the amount of principal outstanding actually diminished each month, the $6 fee (supposed 6 percent rate) amounted to a real interest charge of 11.4 percent of the amount of principal that the borrower actually had over the entire course of the year. That 11.4 percent is the APR.

Obviously, consumer activists wanted the standard use of the APR because it is more accurate. But some consumers may want to be able to calculate the dollar cost of the APR. For them, we've provided a formula in Appendix 2. It also explains the add-on and discount loans, both of which were to have been replaced by the APR.

If you are shopping for a loan and are cited what seems to be a surprisingly low rate, ask the prospective lender if that is the APR. It almost certainly isn't. Some lenders persist in citing the add-on or discount rates on the grounds that they are more comprehensible to the borrower. With the widespread use of the APR these days, these old rates merely serve to confuse matters.

The APR is supposed to include not only the basic finance charge but any other fees. If the lender is paid an extra percentage point during the first year as a fee for the administrative costs of the loan or if a charge is made to cover an investigation of your credit standing, both should be included in the APR. When the add-on rate was used, such charges were often levied separately.

Usually a loan is repaid by level, monthly payments. Some lenders offer loans on which interest or perhaps a small portion or principal is repaid in each regular payment. The bulk of the principal is left for the final payment. This kind of loan, not too frequent now, is an open invitation, if not a requirement, to refinance the loan and start all over again. This loan is likely to be much more in the interest of the lender than the borrower.

Does It Pay to Prepay?

Because consumer loans are generally small, a change in the borrower's circumstances may well lead to an attempt to prepay the loan. While it may seem fair and even obvious that full repayment of the loan should mean the end of interest payments, the penalties for prepayment may actually be considerable.

The penalty may come either in the form of a flat fee or as a result of the computation method used by the bank. In theory, a flat fee should be charged only when a loan is prepaid in the first month or two. In such a case, the bank has probably not received enough interest income to cover its costs in setting up the loan. But some banks may insist on a prepayment penalty fee at any time the loan is paid off before its term.

You may recall that both the add-on and discount methods of calculating interest do not accurately reflect the amount of interest you may owe at any particular moment during the life of a loan. If you decide to prepay, how does the bank know how much interest you have paid to that point? Chances are, the bank uses a method called "the Rule of 78s."

The Rule of 78s is based on the notion of a loan paid off in 12 equal monthly payments. The loan is deemed to be composed of 12 principal parts in the first month. Twelve installment units are payable that month, one for each part. In the second month, when one-twelfth of the principal has been repaid, 11 principal parts and 11 installment units remain. Each month, the number of installment units decreases by one. Over the twelve months there are a total of 78 installment units. (The "Rule" can be extended to any number of months.)

If a loan is prepaid at the end of the first month, the borrower is considered to have used 12 installment units. Therefore, he or she must pay 12/78s of the total finance charge. That means that more than 15 percent of all the interest that must be paid on the loan is due for just a little more than 8 percent of the time the loan was outstanding. In the second month, 11/78s must be paid in addition to the 12/78s paid as interest in the first month.

Obviously, the Rule of 78s is not exact. It dates from precomputer days when it was just about the best a bank could do. It is roughly fair when used in conjunction with the add-on or discount methods of computing interest. It is most unfair in the early stages of a loan. At those stages, the bank is paid more interest than it has actually earned. The Rule of 78s is not illegal, but lenders are now required to inform borrowers in advance just how much of a penalty is built into the loan in case of prepayment. San Francisco Consumer Action has calculated that "with a $3,000, 36-month loan and a total finance charge of $585.00 (APR 11.96 percent), the penalty under the Rule of 78s for prepayment after three months would be about $7.00." As loans get larger, the prepayment penalty using this method can be substantial.

The best prepayment method for the consumer and the one most likely to be used if the loan is actually calculated using the APR is the "actuarial" method. The bank can calculate exactly how much interest is due at the time of any given payment. If the borrower pays the interest on the loan for the period he or she has actually held the loan, plus whatever remains outstanding of the principal, there are simply no additional interest payments. That amounts to making a payment when it is due and then returning the rest of the principal. As banks have begun shifting over to actual calculation by the APR method, they have begun dropping prepayment penalties.

Truth or Consequences

The Truth-in-Lending law was designed to ensure that borrowers could compare the cost of loans and, in general, know what they were getting themselves into. Unfortunately, the law is frequently violated, in part because borrowers do not know of its requirements.

Banks and other lenders are forbidden to quote add-on or discount rates that give the inaccurate impression of a low rate of interest. They are required to give the APR, or simple interest rate. In many cases, however, the same "low" rates are quoted as previously, thus putting the honest lenders at a great disadvantage because they quote the "higher" APR.

The potential borrower should ask specifically if the rate quoted is the APR and accept nothing other than a direct affirmative answer. If you don't get the proper answer, the bank should be reported to the Federal Reserve Board, which is responsible for national enforcement of the Truth-in-Lending law. In some states, the law is under the administration of the state, and you should be on the safe side by submitting a complaint to the state banking department as well as to the Federal Reserve. For nonbank lenders, complaints should go to the Federal Trade Commission. Failure to provide you with APR information is a violation of the law, and almost all banks will provide the proper information if they see that you know exactly what you want.

Another requirement of the law is that all charges in addition to the principal be figured into the APR. That means that you need not pay any amount that the lender claims in addition to the finance charges. Such charges would, of course, actually push up the effective interest rate, which is not permitted.

Information on prepayment penalties is also supposed to be provided by the lender before the loan is made. San Francisco Consumer Action has found that a typical disclosure statement reads:

> If the loan is paid in full prior to maturity, borrower shall receive a rebate of any precomputed interest in the finance charge according to the Rule of 78s; provided, however, that there will first be deducted therefrom the sum of $25.

The borrower has to pick his or her way through this jargon in order to understand the prepayment clause. "Precomputed interest" refers to the finance charge that is added to the principal at the initiation of the loan. In short, if the principal is $1,000 and the finance charge is $200, thus requiring repayment of $1,200, the $200 constitutes precomputed interest.

The "rebate" is not actually paid to the borrower. Instead, the credit or interest that is due as a result of prepayment is applied against the outstanding amount of the loan. That may mean that the borrower has to return less to the lender.

If, for example, the $1,000 loan is paid back in one month, by the Rule of 78s the amount of interest due is 12/78 of $200, or $30.77. That leaves a rebate of $169.23. At the end of the first month, the borrower must thus pay $1,030.77. There is no actual cash return to him. This amount is further increased by the flat fee of $25, making the total payment $1,055.77. Interest of 5.6 percent will have been paid for the month—67 percent annual interest. Only the existence of interest-rate ceilings in the law actually prevents the interest rate from reaching this point. Yet this example indicates just how prepayment penalties can push effective interest more than three times as high as the apparent rate. That's why it's important for the borrower to know exactly what the prepayment penalties are.

The High Cost of Money

In addition to interest rates and the methods of calculating them, a number of other factors push up the cost of borrowed money.

Many lenders charge a late fee if any specific installment payment is more than 10 or 15 days late. The charge is often 5 percent of the amount of the overdue monthly payment, including both principal and interest. This late charge is added to the monthly installment and can obviously drive the cost of the loan up. If it is not paid, it may hasten the moment when the loan goes into default.

In the case of APR or simple-interest loans as they may be called, the bank should calculate the interest due on the basis of the actual period of time the money was on loan. Thus, if the payments are made late, that will drive up interest costs because the principal has been held longer. Some banks will charge a late fee as well, but there is no justification for such a charge. The bank is assured of full compensation for the money it has lent, because it charges interest for each day the loan is outstanding.

By the same token, if you make payments ahead of the agreed schedule, you should be charged less interest. Whatever you do, the amount of the installment payments should be level, unless you make a special deal. Only the last payment, which will take care of any remaining interest, may differ.

Some banks require people to whom they lend money to have an account with them. While they claim that such an account establishes a relationship with the borrower, making him or her a customer of the bank and hence a favored loan client, these tie-ins boost the interest rate. Of course, such a request is normal for a credit union, which is generally permitted to do business only with its members. In addition, if you have actually banked at the same place for some time, you may be better known as a loan client and eligible for better treatment than a person off the street.

By depositing some of your money in an account at a bank where you borrow money as a result of a tie-in, you do not actually take from the bank all of the principal you have borrowed. In effect, the loan principal is deposited with the bank until it is used. Even if the loan is used immediately, the total amount is reduced, from the bank's point of view, by the balance in your new account. If, for example, you borrow $1,000 at 14.8 percent APR, you might be required to open a checking account with an average balance of $100. The actual net amount that you would have taken from the bank would be only $900. But you are paying interest on $1,000. That would make the actual APR about 16.4 percent.

What's more, checking or savings accounts in the same bank where a loan was made may create the right of offset. The bank can withdraw from that account any amount due on a loan without recourse either to a court or to the borrower. The failure to notify the account holder may put him or her in an embarrassing situation from inadvertently overdrawing the account. This right can create actual added costs and a lot of anguish for the borrower.

If property is pledged as security for a loan, it may be possible for the bank to repossess it without any court action or notice to the borrower. In particular, cars purchased with auto loans are natural targets for such bank action, since they can be picked up right on the street.

The bank may also require that property used as security be insured, and will provide the insurance, with payments as part of the finance charge. These premiums can be high and certainly they profit the lender who gets a cut of them. It's wise for the borrower to shop around for the lowest-cost insurance. The bank cannot require that the insurance be purchased under its auspices.

Your Money or Your Life

The bank can require that the borrower purchase insurance that will guarantee repayment in case he or she is disabled or dies. Credit life insurance fees, if they are paid through the bank, must be included in the APR. Because this pushes up the rate the bank must quote, some have dropped their insistence that credit life insurance be obtained through them.

When banks have sold such insurance, the premiums have often been unusually high. A rate of 50 to 75 cents per $100 of initial indebtedness is common. And Federal statistics indicate that as many as 95 percent of borrowers do purchase credit life insurance from the lender—finance company or bank.

Perhaps the greatest abuse of credit life insurance is that the borrower is required to buy a lot of unnecessary coverage. The face value of the insurance may be the sum of the principal and all of the finance charges over the life of the loan. Yet were the borrower to die before the loan was fully repaid, all of the principal but only a part of the finance charges would actually be due. Admittedly, the amount of insurance declines as the amount of the outstanding balance declines, but it still covers all of the finance charges at any one time.

Most credit life insurance covers the principal amount of the loan, all interest to be paid, the single premium to be paid for insurance, and any other elements of the finance charges. In case of death, any overpayment on the single premium is not refunded. Thus, if the borrower dies early in the life of the loan, the insurance premium is astronomical.

Although credit life insurance offerings are approved and rates are set by state statute or by state insurance department regulations, the actual premium rates and coverage vary. For example, some companies offer an extended benefit period so that if you fall somewhat behind in your loan payments before the loan term draws to a close, you have a better chance of remaining insured.

You may always go to an insurance company and request exactly the insurance policy you need to cover the bank's specifications. Comparison shopping among insurance companies is advisable. In any case, you should always carry sufficient life insurance coverage to protect your survivors from a burden of debt. But the decision on what kind of and how much insurance you need should not be made at the loan officer's desk in the bank. For example, buying term coverage through Savings Bank Life Insurance, where it is available, is almost certain to be less expensive than credit life.

If you purchase a policy from an insurance company, you will gain advantages further reducing the cost that are not available with credit life insurance bought through a bank. The premium for credit life insurance is set in terms of the amount being financed and does not take into consideration the age, or health of the borrower (credit life insurance is not available for borrowers over age sixty-five). Commercial life insurance always takes age into account and may also require a physical examination. Because such flexibility is absent in credit life policies, the younger subsidize the older borrowers.

Unlike mutual life and savings bank life policies, credit life pays no dividend based on the experience of all those insured. Thus, if there is a particularly low payout by credit life, that simply means more profit for the insurer. Indeed, credit life insurers often share their gains with the banks that have sold such profitable insurance.

Get a Horse

Perhaps the most frequent purpose of a consumer loan is for the purchase of an automobile. Banks like to make this kind of loan because it will be secured by the car itself. Even if you borrow the money directly from the automobile dealer, he will probably transfer your debt to the bank, making you ultimately the bank's customer.

If you borrow from the dealer and he's sold you a

clinker, you may be able to use the threat of nonpayment as a weapon for getting him to fulfill his part of the bargain. In some arrangements that dealers make with banks, he must repurchase all loan contracts in default. In order to avoid this situation, he may be willing to meet your demands to repair the buggy. But in many arrangements, the dealer simply sells the note to the bank, which will have to repossess in case of default.

If you borrow the necessary funds from a bank, you cannot use the withholding of payments as a way of influencing the dealer. You should weigh this disadvantage against a major advantage in borrowing from the bank: If you eliminate the dealer as a middleman when you borrow, the finance charges are likely to be considerably lower. It's always wise to acquire competitive information from the dealer where you may purchase a car and from the bank where you may borrow the money. Both should be willing to provide you the information without your being obligated. If they insist on your making a commitment before they provide the information, go elsewhere.

Until recently, the maximum term for automobile loans was 36 months. Because of inflation, which pushes auto prices up, and recession, which limited purchasers' ability to pay, such loans may now run as long as 48 months. The longer the loan, the greater the total interest paid, and with high rates the difference can be substantial.

Education Loans: A Good Deal

A wide variety of education loans and grants are available, many of them administered directly by the college or university. But banks also participate in a loan program that offers the borrower a good deal.

The program was initiated by New York State in 1958 and was later adopted by the U.S. Department of Health, Education and Welfare. Loans are made to the residents of the state where the bank is located for use at any regionally accredited institution anywhere. In New York, loans used for vocational training must be used in-state.

If a family's total income minus an allowance of 10 percent is less than $15,000 a year, the Federal government will pay all finance charges until nine months after graduation. At that point, the borrower must begin to repay the loan at an annual rate of 7 percent. When the adjusted family income is between $15,000 and $30,000, the state pays 4 percent of the interest and the borrower's family pays 3 percent. Repayment of the loan begins immediately, even while the student is still in school.

The 7-percent rate is obviously well below the recent commercial rates. That's because of the government repayment guarantees. For college loans, 80 percent of any bank loss on a loan would be paid by HEW and 20 percent by the state.

The New York experience shows a loan loss of 4.6 percent of the dollar value. Chase Manhattan Bank, which is an active participant in the program, has reported that their defaults have risen during the last five years. New York State officials maintain that the delinquency rate has not increased significantly. A Chase officer also reported that the terms for making loans have been liberalized. He also noted that students' families appear to regard the loans as something of a grant and make inadequate psychological and financial preparations to make the monthly loan payments.

These guaranteed loans are far more attractive than a normal consumer loan. For those with limited resources, these loans may be the only way of assuring their children a college education. The potential borrower should inquire at the bank about such a loan well in advance of the time it would be needed. And watch out for education loans that amount to nothing more than personal loans. For example, Chemical Bank published a brochure on education loans, offered at 14.21 percent APR, without including a word about the benefits of the New York State Higher Education loan for families with incomes between $15,000 and

$30,000. In fact, Chemical makes it seem that the guaranteed-loan program only covers families with incomes up to $15,000.

The Discriminating Lender

Some people have no trouble with loans because they simply cannot obtain them. Whatever the guarantees of the Constitution and laws, members of minority groups, young people and women have found themselves the victims of discrimination. Supposedly, loan officers base their rejection of such people on an appraisal that they probably will be unable to repay. But that appraisal itself may be based on outmoded prejudices about the financial responsibility of such people.

While general provisions of the law were designed to ensure fair treatment of all groups, there was little specific protection built into the law. Lenders would often go on considerable lengths to disguise the grounds of their discrimination against minority group members and young people. But they were amazingly frank in their refusal to grant credit to women on equal terms with men. Apparently, their attitude is motivated by the belief that because women can become pregnant and hence interrupt their work, they cannot be considered as reliable as men, who are saved by biology more than by any supposed superior capacity to manage their financial affairs.

The Equal Credit Opportunity Act, which entered into effect in October 1975, is designed to abolish this outmoded discrimination on the basis of sex. The new law specifically bans discrimination on the basis of sex or marital status in all kinds of credit transactions. Among banks and thrifts, the only institutions not covered are the few state banks that are neither Federally insured nor members of the Federal Reserve System.

Under the law, an installment loan application is prescribed, with questions limited to financial background, employment, residence, and security for the loan. No questions may be asked about a spouse's financial status unless that person wishes to be a co-signer. A rejection form is also required, to be used if you are turned down. The only valid grounds for refusal relate to credit record, employment status, income, residency, and a negative report from a credit office or other consumer reporting agency. If the last reason is cited, you are entitled to obtain a copy of that report. After a slow start, regulators are now inspecting to make sure the appropriate forms are properly used.

The Equal Credit Opportunity Act rules out all of these forms of discrimination. If they are encountered, the borrower should take the matter up with the appropriate Federal regulatory agency (see Chapter 8). The Federal Reserve has the ultimate rule-making authority.

Women have used credit less often than men, so they may not have established credit records. For a married couple, the husband may simply have signed for all of the loans. Generally, maintaining checking or savings accounts or a credit-card account should be sufficient to satisfy most banks. Consumers Union suggests that women take out a loan that they don't need and then repay it as a way of creating a credit record. Yet this is both unreasonable and wasteful and will tend only to accentuate the arbitrary standards maintained by some banks. Indeed, a woman should need to prove only that she has no adverse credit experience and that she has the capacity to repay comparable to that required of men. Any other requirement for obtaining credit is not in the consumer's interest and may be against the law.

Discrimination on the basis of race, age, religion, national origin, and receipt of income from public assistance has been banned since March 1977.

To Have and to Hold

Banks may become involved in credit transactions without the consumer's being immediately aware of their role. If the consumer makes a purchase and finances it on credit extended by the merchant, the note may be "discounted" by a bank. That means that the bank pays the merchant less than the amount of the loan but relieves him of the further need of trying to collect what's due.

As a result, the consumer will actually be paying the bank even though the original deal was made with the merchant. If the goods purchased prove to be defective or even worthless, the bank will still want to be paid and will take action to get you to make the required payments.

The bank cannot be held responsible for the merchant's failure to sell a good product, because it is the holder-in-due-course of the loan. The law presumes that the bank cannot be aware of the merchant's failure to perform his part of the deal and is once removed from him. In effect, the law requires you to pay for a product that may never have been delivered. In case of difficulty, the purchaser must have direct recourse to the merchant. Only with regard to credit-card sales does Federal law sweep aside the holder-in-due-course doctrine.

The lesson is not to believe that if you are dissatisfied with a product, you can have the matter taken care of by withholding payment on the loan. That may only complicate the situation further.

The Collector

Just as banks sometimes discriminate against people who are fully qualified to borrow, they also make it too easy for people who should not go deeply into debt. Loan officers get ahead by making loans, and it is often easiest to "sell" a loan to a person in tight financial straits. The prospect of a loan to consolidate debts may be irresistible. The loan officer may give very little thought to the sacrifices the borrower will have to make in order to repay the loan, or, more seriously, to the real possibility of default.

The Nader study of New York's Citibank provides the best documentation available on the fate of the low-income borrower. Citibank is widely considered, in the banking business, to be the best-managed bank. Its assets have risen sharply, due, in part, to its willingness to make loans that other banks would consider too risky.

According to the study, Citibank approved 85 percent of the loan applications made. The result was that 11 percent of all consumer loans were made to people with incomes below $6,000 a year. Citibank and other lenders generally use a guideline indicating that a person should not devote more than 20 percent of his or her income to the repayment of debts, exclusive of mortgage payments. For low-income people, Citibank reportedly believes this guideline should be lowered to 15 percent. In actual practice, the guideline appears to be ignored, and Citibank often winds up in court, having brought suit against the low-income borrower. More than two-thirds of all court actions on loan defaults conducted by Citibank are directed against those with incomes below $6,000.

Professor David Caplovitz of Columbia University prepared a study in 1970 that documented the way in which Citibank led low-income people into debt. To cite just one example: A man owed $1,200 to the Beneficial Finance, $800 on his credit card, $150 to the Columbia Record Club, and $90 to Manufacturers Hanover. Although his income was only $6,300 a year, he received a personal loan of $1,000 from Citibank, plus a credit card with which he ran up another $1,000 in debts. Since the Citibank loan was not used to pay off his other debts, to meet all of these payments took more than $150 a month. The 15-percent guideline figure was $77, and the 20 percent limit was $105.

Critics may question whether this man revealed his debt situation when he took out the loan. Actually, it was up to the bank to determine his total indebtedness. Perhaps the question ought to be: Did the bank ask him about his debts? If it did, the loan should not have been made.

In some cases, the amount of the monthly payments was allowed to go as high as 60 percent of income. Obviously, people have a hard time meeting such payments. If they have borrowed from Citibank and have defaulted, they may find themselves in New York City Civil Court. But first they will be subjected to the threats and abuse of the collection system. Not only will a borrower receive a series of letters threatening the most dire consequences, but he or she may be subject to abuse. The Nader study reports on one phone call from the bank that has become a classic in the literature:

"Mr. Jones?"

"No. This is his roommate."

"Is Mr. Jones there?"

"No."

"I don't believe you."

"Who's this?"

"This is First National City Bank. Mr. Jones owes us five hundred dollars, and we want our money or he'll be in trouble. Tell Jones to call us as soon as he gets in."

"Can't you be more polite?"

"Mind your own fucking business." *(Click.)*

Most people are afraid that the bank will go to their employer or garnishee their wages. In many places, you cannot lose your job for that reason, but the law is seldom enforced. The Caplovitz study found that in 46 percent of the cases studied, the employer was contacted, and in 10 percent, the borrower lost his or her job. This threat is a powerful incentive to repayment. As a result, the borrower may take out a new loan in order to postpone a confrontation with his employer.

As a last resort, but one that Citibank uses frequently, the borrower is brought to court. Of course, it is possible that he or she does not even know that the bank has filed a legal action because the process server who is supposed to deliver the court notice may never have done so. Investigations have revealed that they often make only a halfhearted effort. And even if the borrower does make it to court, he or she is likely to face all of the legal talent the bank feels is necessary to win its case. Professor Caplovitz found that half of those defaulting earn less than $5,000, so their chances of engaging competent legal counsel are slim. They may go to the OEO legal service office, a community legal operation funded by the Federal government. In fact, either because they never get word or because they know the case is hopeless, most debtors do not show up in court and the bank automatically wins its case. In this way, Citibank uses the courts as a collection agency.

The story of Citibank is obviously not the case of all banks. Others, less intent on rapid expansion, are more careful in examining the borrower's ability to repay. As a result, they turn away low-income customers. In fact, to the extent that Citibank makes loans to low-income people, it is to be praised. Its great failing appears to come from lending them more money than the bank's own guideline indicates is proper.

The Friendly Finance Company

The borrower's last resort is the finance company. It will provide a loan to a person who expected to have a hard time getting one from the bank. In return, the finance company will charge the maximum interest the law will allow.

The finance company is, in many cases, merely an extension of the bank itself. Because finance companies do not have depositors, they turn to the bank for their funds. They must pay whatever rate the bank may require, which can drive up the cost of their funds. Actually, such giants as Household Finance or Beneficial Finance have good standing with the banks because they repay their loans.

Finance-company rates are kept in check by legal limits. They may go as high as 45 percent on loans of less than $300. At the end of 1976, the national average rate for personal loans by finance companies was 20.86 percent, more than half again higher than the rates charged by commercial banks. With the need for the companies themselves to borrow from a bank, and a default rate about double that at banks, such high rates are not surprising.

What may be surprising is the number of people who are willing to pay those rates. About 22 percent of all installment credit is obtained from finance companies. People are actually driven to use the finance companies by banks that do not want to assume the risk of loans to low-income people but are willing to provide the capital.

Not all people who use finance companies are the very poor. Some people prefer the atmosphere of the finance company, which operates out of a neighborhood storefront, to the cold and impressive formality of a bank. On the National Educational Television program "Banks and the Poor," Schuyler Barrack, of the Harlem Legal Aid Society, described what happens:

> Nowadays more than before, he first goes to a bank. But I'm afraid when he goes, he doesn't find the kind of reception he finds in other places. I've witnessed them. I think we all have—the loan officer gives him an application to fill out. Frankly, it's weighted against him. He takes it home and reads the questions. The questions don't apply to him. They ask how long he's lived in his apartment, he's not very stable there. It asks about property he owns, he doesn't own any property. If he has a car, he doesn't have any real equity in the car. In other words, he has very little besides his word and his promise to pay this loan back. Most often he does not come back with that loan application, and if he does, he knows he's going to face an unfriendly reception. The questions have told him that, so he turns to an alternative. The alternative is the small loan company. They don't start with a form, they start with a friendly face-to-face reception. If he's Spanish, they have a Spanish-speaking person in the office. If he's black, there are black people in the office. They want him to feel at home.

In addition to those whom the banks would consider marginal borrowers, many middle- and upper-income people feel more comfortable with a loan company. Maybe they fear that a credit check by the bank would reveal a past event they would just as soon keep quiet. Perhaps they believe that they will simply not have to bare as much of their financial history to a loan company as to a bank. Possibly they believe they have already borrowed all the bank will give them. Or they simply prefer the atmosphere of a loan company. Finally, in many cases, borrowers believe the banks would refuse them when, in fact, they would not.

Finance companies are often criticized as harmful to the consumer interest because of their high rates and their ready willingness to extend loans even if their borrowers are unable to repay. They merit such criticism when they willfully disguise the high interest payments instead of honestly stating the rate. Some carefully avoid any indication of the total finance charge as opposed to the monthly fee for fear that the customer will decide against taking the loan.

In some places such as Arkansas and the District of Columbia, finance companies have been driven out of the market because of the alleged harm they do consumers. This has been accomplished by denying them the right to charge sufficiently high interest to cover their losses on defaulted loans. Banks may actually have given their quiet support to the antifinance-company movement in these and other places. They will then pick up those customers who would, in any case, have been eligible for bank loans. What happens to the others? Some will travel considerable distances to patronize finance companies in neighboring states. Others will turn to the illegal loan market—to the loan sharks who can charge rates that are totally uncontrolled by law. Finally, some, who would have been able to repay a finance company loan, will simply be unable to obtain credit.

In short, the consumer-oriented push to shut down finance companies can result in some people having to pay higher rates, others having their freedom of choice limited, and still others being prevented from having any chance at all for a loan.

There is nothing illegal about the way many reputable finance companies operate. They have evolved as a part of the credit system to meet a real need. As *Consumer Reports* notes: "Their rates reflect the characteristics of their customers."

On the basis of rates alone, you should try a bank before turning to a finance company. If you do seek a loan from a finance company, remember that the rates will be high, particularly for a small loan. In any case, insist on knowing the APR. The finance company may prefer to cite only the amount of each installment payment. That's useful to know in calculating whether you can afford the loan according to the 20-percent guideline, but it will not allow you to compare the cost of the loan with that of another finance company or other credit source.

Some finance companies can be unscrupulous—charging too much and disclosing too little. And some are relentless in their harassment of slow payers or "deadbeats." Some try to pressure customers to get deeper into debt, and thus extend the loan-repayment period, or to take a new loan. Such tactics may result in the borrower's permanent financial bondage. As a result, most states supervise finance company operations closely.

In short, try to avoid using a finance company, but if you do, handle with care. In case of any difficulty with one, contact your state or local consumer affairs office, the state attorney general, or the state banking department.

The Loan Checklist

Most people have an immediate need for the money they seek to borrow. They feel, in part as a result of the application procedure, that they will be lucky to get the loan. All too often, they fail to recognize that most financial institutions eagerly solicit their business because it means profits. But even though a bank is eager to lend you money, you should be careful to investigate any loan.

1. It may be preferable to save in advance rather than to borrow. Consider the alternatives. Of course, waiting to make a purchase while the needed money is accumulated may mean that the ultimate price is higher due to inflation.

2. Shop around for interest rates. There are great differences in the rates charged, although direct competition among institutions may seem to be lacking. You should investigate the charges and conditions of commercial banks not only as compared with thrifts and other institutions, but even among the commercial banks themselves. In the same city, significant savings can be realized. Indeed, even within the same bank a customer may be able to obtain two different rate quotations from two different loan officers.

3. Join a credit union if you are eligible. Not only will

you receive a reasonably good return on your savings, but you will be able to obtain loans easily and on good terms. Indeed, as an essentially cooperative undertaking, a credit union may even rebate a part of your interest charges. Another advantage of a credit union is that the member is more often remembered as an individual than he would be in a big bank. Personal attention adds to the appeal of these institutions.

4. When applying for a loan, prepare the answers to all of the obvious questions well in advance. Loan officers may look upon your uncertainty as a sign that they should question your ability to repay. Confidence on the part of the borrower will make a better impression. Where there is an explanation for circumstances such as a recent change of address, do not hesitate to volunteer all relevant facts when answering a question orally or in writing. Don't be on the defensive.

5. Insist on knowing the APR for the loan. There is no need to agree to anything until you have full information on the rate and other conditions. When an interest rate is cited, if it seems unusually low, mention that and check that you are being given the APR. You should also inquire as to the amount of the monthly payments. While the APR will help you compare with other possible sources, the actual payment amounts will help you determine whether you can afford the loan.

6. You should be informed about any prepayment penalty in whatever form it is levied. Even if you do not intend to pay off the loan early, circumstances may change later. Try to bargain for the deletion of any prepayment penalty. If interest is calculated on the add-on or discount basis, you may have to settle for the Rule of 78s, but you should certainly avoid paying any other penalty if at all possible. If simple interest or the APR is used to calculate how much is due, there is no need for any penalty, except when the loan is repaid quite early in its life. Then interest may not actually cover bank costs. Try to avoid a prepayment penalty that is unwarranted.

7. Check on all other fees and make sure they are included in the calculation of the APR. Watch out also for

tie-in arrangements such as the requirement to open a checking or savings account. Inquire if the bank uses an offset that allows it to take money out of your account to meet a loan charge. If there is both a tie-in and an offset, keep shopping. Perhaps the bank will accept your opening a savings account, while it gives up the automatic offset right. It would have to obtain a court order before it could touch the money in your savings account to meet a loan payment. That's a lot better protection for the consumer, and yet it gives the bank reasonable assurance that there is a degree of security for its loan.

8. Avoid the purchase of credit life insurance if it is at all possible. If you need insurance on your life because you have contracted a loan, shop around the insurance companies, especially the one that has already written a policy on your life. While life insurance may not always be a bargain, it is likely to be more economical than credit life. Since you should always maintain an adequate amount of life insurance, you may not need to purchase another policy if you take out a loan.

9. If you take a loan to purchase an automobile, be sure to compare the various dealer plans and what you can obtain at a bank or thrift institution. Few people are in urgent need of a car when they make a purchase, and unless you are, you should not allow yourself to be rushed by any salesman. If the dealer promises to save you paperwork, find out just how much there is and then determine if the services are worth the price differential.

10. If you feel you are the victim of discrimination in connection with a loan, tell the lender directly and let him know you intend to take further action. That may be enough to bring about a change in his attitude. If not, write him formally, with a copy to your local or state consumer department, the state attorney general, the state banking department, and the Federal Reserve Board. That may bring results.

11. Beware of the holder-in-due-course doctrine. Do not count on being able to settle your differences with a merchant by withholding payments from the bank or other

institution where you borrowed the money to make a purchase. While this rule, which separates the debt from the seller, is being whittled down, it is still the law and must be accepted.

12. Don't take a loan unless you can afford it. The guideline of not taking on a total debt, exclusive of mortgage, of more than 20 percent of income is absolutely sound. Failure to observe the guideline could bring financial disaster. When estimating income, it's wise not to include overtime or work on the side if these sources of income are not pretty certain.

13. If it's at all possible, avoid using a finance company. Their rates are simply too high to make a loan attractive. If, for any reason, you decide to go ahead with one, you should ask questions about rates, duration, amount of payments, prepayments, and all of the other matters peculiar to a loan. Many loan companies are reputably run, but this is one area where the borrower should remain alert and be satisfied before taking the loan that all relevant questions now or later are answered.

14. If you find yourself over your head in debt, you may be advised to seek help from a credit counselor. Consumers Union suggests contacting the National Foundation for Consumer Credit in Washington, D.C., which maintains a list of 167 nonprofit credit-counseling centers. But be careful. Most credit counselors are, in fact, financed by the very institutions that hold your debt. Obviously, they want to protect their loan. Once again, it's worth asking what relationship, if any, a credit counselor has with banks and other lenders. If the counselor is supported by banks, he or she will want to devise a way for you to repay your debt fully. Perhaps the sacrifice required to do this is too great. In that case, you should consider bankruptcy, which allows you to settle your debts by paying less than 100 cents on the dollar. Bankruptcy may be the only way to get your personal financial affairs on a sound footing again. Few credit counselors will advise this course of action. You would have to consult a lawyer if you wanted to consider this course.

6 Mortgaging Your Future

A mortgage loan is almost certainly the largest loan you'll ever take. While you may borrow money to buy a home from another member of the family or from a credit union or even from a life insurance company, you are most likely to obtain the mortgage from a bank or a thrift institution. About three-quarters of all mortgages on one- to four-family dwellings and on farms were held, on December 31, 1976 by these financial institutions and life insurance companies. Among these, the savings and loans held the lion's share:

Savings and loans	55.1%
Commercial banks	20.4%
Mutual savings banks	15.3%
Life insurance companies	9.2%

This means that in most parts of the country you are most likely to obtain your mortgage from either a savings and loan or a commercial bank. Because of their concentration in certain Eastern states, savings banks are the predominant source of mortgage money for individuals in such states as New York, Massachusetts, New Hampshire, and Maine.

The savings and loans have virtually exploded on the scene within the past thirty years to meet the need for mortgage money to service the post–World War II housing boom. Returning veterans wanted a home of their own, and the rising expectations of many city dwellers have been best exemplified by the desire for a home in the suburbs.

The expansion of savings and loans was directly tied to

the increased demand for housing because they are, in fact, highly specialized in the mortgage business. Mortgages represent some 84 percent of their total assets.

Historically, although not now, savings and loans have been able to pay more for their deposits—the money they need to lend for mortgages. Their ability to pay more for their money resulted from their mortgage loan charges, which are somewhat higher than those of other institutions.

They specialize in so-called conventional mortgages, those which do not benefit from any Federal government guarantee. Government-backed mortgages are subject to interest ceilings imposed by the agency making the guarantee. Conventional mortgages are limited only by state law.

Another factor that has made savings and loans popular is their close relationship to their community. They make most of their loans right in their neighborhood and are thus in a unique position to know their borrower. Not only are they in a good position to evaluate risk, but they remain involved in the mortgage-making and -servicing business throughout the life of the loan.

Commercial banks were attracted increasingly into the mortgage business by the expansion of government guarantees. The Federal Housing Administration (FHA) program began in 1934, and the Veterans Administration (VA) guarantees after World War II enabled banks to make mortgages secure in the knowledge that they could be bailed out in case of bad judgment. In addition, the rate of return on mortgages was better than on other possible investments. Such loans are now a major profit line for commercial banks. in 1975, for example, large banks reported that money cost them only a 4.6-percent interest rate but that they received 8.2 percent on mortgage notes (Of course, banks obtained much of their funds from low-interest savings accounts, and those mortgages include commercial properties in which the banks specialize.) Finally, with increased acceptance of the idea of one-stop banking, more people have put their funds into savings accounts at commercial banks, thus providing more mortgage money.

Not all commercial banks are interested in making residential loans, and even fewer back multifamily dwellings. The Nader study of New York's Citibank reveals that institution's reluctance to get involved in the mortgage business for housing. Only 2 percent of the bank's assets go for residential mortgages. Citibank reportedly specializes in single-family dwellings, not the prime form of housing in its area. That's because the bank extends mortgage loans as an accommodation to employees of its major corporate clients. As for apartment buildings, especially in areas of New York that need to be renewed, Citibank stays away as much as possible.

The situation is not much better for commercial banks as a whole. About 9 percent of the assets of all commercial banks are made up of farm and small-family residence loans. Obviously, commercial banks prefer to concentrate on commercial properties. For those residential mortgage loans they do make, commercial banks usually ask for bigger down payments than do the thrifts.

Mutual savings banks date from the early nineteenth century. In contrast with savings and loans, which grew to meet the need for loans, savings banks developed to meet the need for a safe place to deposit funds. They did not spread far off the Eastern seaboard as the nation developed, but those banks which were formed have become a major part of the mortgage scene.

Conservative in their lending policies, they fared better during the Great Depression than did other institutions holding mortgages. Mutual savings banks not only operate on their home turf, but also act to allocate mortgage money to high-need areas. Their officers actively search for such places to invest their banks' funds.

Life insurance companies generally purchase mortgages from banks, so the individual is unlikely to come in contact with one in connection with the purchase of a house.

The choice of an institution for obtaining a mortgage may, of course, be limited. In many areas, there are no savings banks. In others, commercial banks are more interested in mortgage loans than they appear to be in New

York. On an existing house, the mortgage may be held at a thrift that knows the property and is willing to continue the mortgage or originate a new one with the purchaser. But you should check the market whenever you make a real-estate purchase, because loan rates and other conditions may vary. When dealing with loans of this magnitude, small interest-rate differences can amount to thousands of dollars over the life of the mortgage. With a long relationship ahead, the individual will want to seek an institution that is interested in its mortgage business and has experience in handling the kinds of problems that may arise.

Yes, We Have No Money

In the mortgage area, the notion of the financial intermediary, so dear to economists in explaining the banking system, is the most clear. If people have money to save and if they put it in the bank or a thrift, more money will be available for underwriting mortgages. If the economy is prosperous and inflation is moderate, people are likely to have funds available to save. That means "easy money," with the interest rates that banks must pay to attract savings being allowed to slip down. Because they must pay less for funds, they can charge less for mortgages, and there is generally enough money available to finance all mortgage requests.

In recent years, this state of affairs has become a fading memory. First, inflation began to eat into the share of personal income that could be allocated to savings. In addition, the Federal Reserve raised interest rates in an effort to draw some funds into savings. Inflation often means that too much money is seeking to buy too few goods. The Fed's action was designed to ease the inflationary pressure by drawing away some of the money. Unfortunately, that "tight-money" policy is in itself inflationary. Because banks and thrifts have to pay more for the money they attract, they must charge more for the money they lend. The interest rate on mortgages has skyrocketed in the past ten years from less than 5 percent to more than 9 percent. State usury laws, which set a limit on the interest rate for mortgages lower than for other loans, did not rise as fast as the cost of money. When the going rate hit state ceilings, banks ceased issuing mortgages because they could not operate in the black under the ceiling. With less money available, the banks and thrifts had to increase the qualifications they set for mortgage borrowers. In particular, they required that the home purchaser put up a larger share of the cost as a down payment.

Added to inflation were the effects of recession. Individuals simply had less money to spend as production was cut back and they either worked less or were laid off. Obviously, that put a further crimp on savings available to finance mortgages, to say nothing of the problem faced by the unemployed in buying or keeping a home.

While these obvious developments were taking place, thrifts were running into other problems, not so obvious in their cause, but crystal-clear in their effect. Higher interest rates meant that thrifts, in particular, had to face competition for the saver's dollar. Even the Federal government itself offered higher interest rates on Treasury bills than the thrifts were allowed. When people took their funds from the thrifts in order to gain the higher interest paid elsewhere in order to keep pace with inflation, the savings bank and savings and loan faced serious problems in finding deposits to finance mortgage loans.

Banks traditionally borrow short and lend long—they accept deposits for short periods but lend out those funds for long periods. Thus, when people wanted to withdraw funds from the thrifts, it meant that the thrifts had to liquidate some of their mortgages that were bringing in a low rate of return because they had begun years earlier.

Toward the end of 1974, banks and thrifts began to give borrowers big discounts on interest in return for full or partial repayment of low-interest mortgages. For example, Lincoln Savings Bank in Brooklyn reportedly told a customer that it would take $12,831.40 in full payment of the $15,073.07 outstanding on his loan. On a monthly basis, the bank said it would count each $100 above the regular payment as $117.47. Chicago's First Federal Savings and Loan said it would negotiate individual deals. This approach has some benefit for the borrower nearing the end of the loan. Most of each payment is likely to be principal and not interest, which is deductible. As a result, it may be worthwhile to take advantage of the savings possible by advance payment. But some banks will act only if the borrower takes the first step and makes a cut-rate repayment offer.

In short, perhaps more than any other aspect of an individual's relationship with a bank or thrift institution, mortgage loans are directly affected by what's happening in the national economy. As inflation pushes up the purchase price of housing, it also makes it difficult to meet higher down-payment and interest charges. As a result, potential home buyers should seek, as far as possible, to avoid finding themselves in a situation where they must purchase a home at a specific time. For example, if it's possible to delay or accelerate a planned move to another part of the country, you should do so in light of the mortgage situation. Instead, it is preferable to keep an eye on interest rates and make a purchase when they appear to be easing off. Although the maxim seems correct that over the long run, interest rates do not decline, recent history indicates that rates reflect the economic situation. In 1972, a year when inflation dropped below 4 percent, the general interest-rate level was almost 1 percent below the 1970 standard and more than 1.5 percent below the level that would be reached toward the end of 1974, when double-digit inflation prevailed.

Conventional and Unconventional

A mortgage loan is, in most cases, like any other loan, but a lot bigger. Such a loan is called conventional. Where the government steps in to insure or to guarantee the loan, it assumes a special character. In general, the government does not back loans. But it does stand behind certain housing loans as a way of encouraging banks and thrifts to put money into mortgages in order to stimulate the housing market.

For a person who seeks a mortgage, one backed by the government is almost certainly going to be a better deal than a conventional mortgage. It's important to determine eligibility for either FHA or VA mortgages.

The FHA does not itself make loans or build houses; it insures mortgages extended by banks and thrifts to certain individuals. Just how much is available to back mortgages is determined by appropriations of the United States Congress.

The basic requirements for obtaining FHA backing are similar to those a responsible bank or thrift will impose: a good credit record, sufficient cash for a down payment, a regular income sufficient to cover mortgage payments. The FHA also determines if the property is satisfactory and if the price is fair.

The FHA gets involved at the request of the lender; the home buyer may never have direct contact with the government agency.

The maximum interest rate that can be charged by the institution making the mortgage loan is limited by the Federal government. Often, the FHA interest rate will be lower than the conventional rate by perhaps ¼ or ½ of 1 percent. But in addition to the interest, the borrower pays ½ of 1 percent as a mortgage insurance premium. And the bank or thrift may charge an extra fee to bring the interest on an FHA-backed mortgage up to that of the conventional mortgage. In most cases, however, the person selling the house rather than the buyer must pay these "discount points."

The purchaser may have to make a number of other payments. If the price of the house is higher than the FHA evaluation, the FHA guarantee, and thus presumably the mortgage itself, will cover only the amount the FHA certifies. This, in effect, pushes up the amount of the down payment that must be made. There is also an FHA application fee, and under the terms of all FHA-backed mortgages, the monthly mortgage payment must also include a prorated share of fire insurance and other premiums and of local taxes.

The FHA has two plans for insuring mortgages. Mutual mortgage insurance, known as Section 203 insurance, covers mortgages up to $45,000 for a one-family house. The FHA will not insure the full estimated value of the property, the percentage covered decreasing as the value of the house increases. Unless the purchaser is over sixty-two or purchasing a very low-cost, owner-occupied dwelling, he or she must make the down payment in cash. For buyers over sixty or those purchasing homes in remote areas, the down payment can itself be borrowed. Loans are to be repaid in periods of 10, 15, 20, 25, 30, or, in the case of mortgages made before construction, 35 years.

So-called Section 221 insurance is designed for low- and moderate-income families and for those forced to move because of urban renewal or other government action. The terms of such mortgages are generally far more liberal than Section 203–insured loans, with the down payment set as low as $200 and 30 years to repay.

In general, banks and thrifts like FHA loans because they lend a major element of certainty to mortgage loans that are, in other respects, conventional. In addition, banks can sell FHA mortgages to others easily because they are certain of repayment. That means the bank can obtain needed cash more easily with such mortgages than when it has to try to sell its own conventional loans to other financial institutions.

The VA program is a government guarantee or insurance of a mortgage obtained by an eligible veteran. Eligibility varies over the years as Congress acts to determine just who is classified as a veteran. In addition, entitlement extends for varying periods beyond the end of active duty, depending in part on the nature of the service. Any former member of any of the armed forces can apply to the Veterans Administration, submitting discharge records, to obtain a determination of eligibility and length of entitlement. This application need not be done just at the moment when a house purchase is planned. It may be done at any time and actually facilitates the purchase because the veteran has immediate proof that a VA guarantee can be expected.

The guarantee covers $17,500 or 60 percent of a loan, whichever is smaller. Even if the actual mortgage loan is substantially higher, it is considered to be a VA loan. There is no required down payment so long as the sales price does not exceed a price the VA determines to be fair. The veteran must actually live in the house that is purchased with the VA guarantee. The maximum length of the mortgage is 30 years, and the Federal government imposes a ceiling on the interest rate. As with the FHA-insured loans, VA loans generally have a somewhat lower interest rate than is charged on conventional mortgages. Other conditions require that the veteran have fire and other damage insurance and that if the loan extends beyond five years, there be adequate provision for regular repayment of the principal.

About 25 percent of mortgage loans for residences and farms are backed by FHA or VA plans. The percentage is higher in both savings and loans and mutual savings banks than in commercial banks and other financial institutions.

The VA also makes some direct loans to eligible veterans. For those in small towns and rural areas where there is a shortage of housing credit, and particularly where VA-backed loans have not been made recently, direct VA loans can be made. The maximum loan is $25,000. If the cost of the property is below this amount, the VA may require no down payment.

Either before a mortgage is sought or when you begin talking with a bank or thrift, either you or the lender should contact both the FHA and VA to determine possible eligibility. That small amount of effort could be worth thousands of dollars later on.

Mortgage Shopping

Most home purchasers are completely unaware of the variety of mortgage arrangements that is possible. Instead, they accept what the bank suggests, as long as it meets the general goals they have set. Of course, one bank may use only a limited number of approaches, but it may be worth the purchaser's effort to ask the bank to examine other possibilities or to comparison-shop at other banks or thrifts.

The one rule that is pretty generally part of every mortgage is amortization. That means that the principal of the loan will be fully repaid by a certain deadline through periodic installment payments. While repayment of the principal as well as interest may seem obvious, such a provision was not included in many pre-Depression mortgages. Some home buyers who had faithfully made their interest payments were faced with foreclosure when the bank asked for large repayments of principal.

The most common payment plan, used in all FHA and most VA loans, provides for level payments. Also known as the direct-reduction plan, it provides that each month, for the life of the loan, you pay exactly the same amount. That payment is used to pay the interest due on the loan, and whatever is left goes toward reducing the principal. Because the amount of the principal debt is thus decreased each month, the amount of interest due the following month is also reduced. As a result, in each successive monthly payment, a larger share goes to pay off the principal and a smaller share goes to pay interest due.

By a limited-reduction plan, the bank can provide for partial amortization of the debt during the loan's life with a lump-sum payment due at the end of the loan. For example, a borrower could contract for a 10-year loan for $20,000 with annual amortization payments of $1,000. Then, at the end of the loan period, the borrower would be expected to pay the remaining $10,000. Of course, the bank or thrift could arrange for the refinancing of the mortgage loan.

These loans are popularly called "balloon" mortgages. For the life of the loan, payments are just like those of any other mortgage. The major difference is the relatively short life of the loan. In part because the VA requires that any loan for more than five years include an amortization feature for the repayment of principal, balloon mortgages, on which all of the principal is repaid at the end of the period, often run no longer.

The obvious advantage of the balloon mortgage for the bank or thrift is that the interest rate can be adjusted to reflect changing economic conditions, and the institution is thus not forced to accept too low an interest rate for as long as 30 years. For the purchaser, there is always the chance, but a slight one, that interest rates will fall.

When the balloon mortgage comes due, the bank may require full payment, although this is not likely, because it recognizes that you will simply have to obtain a mortgage elsewhere. Instead, a new agreement may be made for another balloon mortgage or perhaps for a long-term mortgage, which is, in effect, payable on demand after the fixed termination date. In practice, the bank does not call in the loan except in case of default. But there is an element of risk. Amortization may not be required under such a mortgage.

Yet another amortization plan calls for each payment to cover a fixed portion of the principal and the interest due on the outstanding balance. This means monthly payments are largest at the beginning and gradually decline until the last payment, which is the remaining installment of the principal. Obviously, this "straight-reduction" plan is not useful to young homeowners with limited incomes. But because the straight-reduction plan is used with well-secured loans due quarterly or semiannually, it may be attractive to professionals such as doctors, lawyers, and architects, whose income comes from fees rather than from a regular paycheck. The longer payment frequencies allow them to take into account wide swings in their income.

Three other specialized forms of mortgage loan have been developed. The "package" mortgage allows the borrower to include the cost of basic household appliances in the amount of the loan. The "open-end" mortgage allows the bank to lend additional amounts on the same mortgage. In general, the additional borrowing cannot exceed the amount of principal already repaid. Finally, a "demand" mortgage is used for houses under construction. It contains neither a fixed maturity nor a plan for repaying the principal. Once construction is completed, the demand mortgage—actually a construction loan—is liquidated and replaced by a standard long-term loan.

Many people believe that the only mortgage is the long-term, level-payment, amortized loan. In fact, a variety of mortgages exists to suit the needs of both the banks and thrifts and the borrowers. Unless the potential borrower asks questions, the lending institution is likely to offer the plan that best suits its interests, given prevailing conditions in the mortgage market. But if a borrower believes that some other mortgage plan might better serve his needs, he should make his own suggestions to the bank.

A Matter of Great Interest

Three principal factors determine the cost of a mortgage loan: the interest rate, the duration of the loan, and the down payment. The lower the rate, the shorter the length of the mortgage; and the smaller the amount borrowed, the lower the cost of borrowing money. Obviously, the reverse is also true.

Carried to its logical extreme, this rule would say that if you didn't borrow any money at all, the charges would be zero. But that may not be as desirable as it sounds. First, you might have to wait quite a long time before you'd saved up enough to buy a house. Second, you would probably be paying rent in the meantime, which could, in fact, all be going toward a mortgage loan. Third, tax laws favor home purchases by providing deductions for the interest paid on the mortgage loan and for the local property taxes. There is no tax deduction for rent. Finally, with the virtual certainty of permanent inflation, the value of the dollar can be expected to decrease over the years. As a result, by promising now to pay back much later, you will be able to make repayment with dollars that are substantially less valuable. Chances are your income will have been keeping pace with inflation, so the portion of your income devoted to mortgage repayment will have decreased over the years. What's more, inflation will probably have boosted the value of your house quite a bit during the life of the mortgage. For all these reasons, it may, in fact, be more desirable to seek a longer-term mortgage.

To give an idea of the effect of the length of a mortgage on the total amount of interest paid, let's take a $30,000 loan at 7 percent for varying intervals:

5 years	$ 5,643 interest
10 years	$11,800 interest
15 years	$18,537 interest
20 years	$25,822 interest
25 years	$33,612 interest
30 years	$41,852 interest

Thus, to borrow $30,000 for 30 years costs $8,240 more than for 25 years. The monthly payment for a level-repayment mortgage over 25 years would be $212.04; over a 30-year period it would be $199.59.

The chief immediate factor that you will have in mind in seeking a mortgage loan is the size of the monthly payment. Most experts say it should be no more than 20 percent of your take-home, not gross, income. It certainly should go no higher than 25 percent. As a result, selecting the length of the loan, on which the bank may accord you some flexibility, can be determined only after you know the interest rate. Look at the impact of rate differences alone on a 25-year, level-repayment mortgage. The payments include both principal and interest.

	$20,000		$30,000		$40,000	
Rate	*Monthly*	*Total*	*Monthly*	*Total*	*Monthly*	*Total*
.05	$116.92	$35,076	$175.38	$52,614	$233.84	$70,152
.06	128.86	38,658	193.29	57,987	257.72	77,316
.07	141.36	42,408	212.04	63,612	282.72	84,816
.08	154.37	46,311	231.55	69,465	308.73	92,619
.09	167.40	50,220	251.76	75,528	335.68	100,704
.095	174.74	52,422	262.11	78,633	349.48	104,844

The difference over 25 years resulting from an increase of one-half a percentage point in interest on a $30,000 loan amounts to $3,105. And if interest were 9 percent instead of 8 percent, you might well find it necessary to extend the mortgage by five years, if you could. The added point would cost you $20.21 each month. The extension would reduce monthly payments by only $10.37, and of course, payments would extend over five more years.

The impact of higher interest rates on the eventual cost of purchasing a home is greatly significant. Only on mortgages bearing relatively low interest and extending no longer than 20 years can you expect to avoid paying twice the amount of the principal borrowed. To this must be added the down payment. In short, shopping for interest rates is worth the effort; but, far more important, waiting awhile until high rates come down is advisable if at all possible. By the same token, a mortgage at a bargain rate, which may be possible if the bank allows you simply to assume an existing mortgage, is definitely worthwhile.

If you want to know how your own prospective purchase compares with others, the Federal Reserve compiles a national average. The average purchase price for a house financed by a conventional mortgage begun in October 1976 was $48,200, with a down payment of 24.8 percent, or $11,954. The mortgage loan, for $35,500, ran for 27.9 years at an interest rate of 9.08 percent. Fees and charges amounting to 1.38 percent of the loan, or $490, were levied. These charges were mostly accounted for by the bank's fees for making a loan.

Let's Make a Deal

When you are ready to make a purchase requiring a mortgage, it's time to shop for a bank or thrift that will provide the loan. Especially in times of tight money, that institution is quite likely to be located in the same community as the new house. As the amount of money available for loans is reduced, banks tend to provide mortgages increasingly as part of their obligation to the local community from which they draw deposits. Having an account at a bank where you seek a mortgage can be an advantage.

The bank or thrift should provide you with a disclosure statement as required by the Truth-in-Lending Act. You should always get one at the time a mortgage loan is made, but when shopping for a mortgage, it is wise to ask for such forms from each lending institution you visit. After all, the legislative purpose in requiring such forms was to give the purchaser the opportunity to make a full and fair comparison.

The disclosure form will indicate the type of mortgage, the amount of the note, the term, and the interest rate. It will also include the amount of each monthly payment, including a balloon payment, if appropriate. Most important, it will include the total of all payments of interest and principal. In addition, data on fire insurance and life insurance may be included. The bank or thrift cannot require you to purchase either through a company they suggest, but it is virtually certain that they will demand that you obtain fire insurance satisfactory to them.

On the disclosure form, the bank or thrift must indicate all finance charges such as their own service and origination fees and title search and all other expenditures relating to the recording of the agreement. In the event the fees included a special interest charge during the first year—designed to cover the administrative costs of making the loan—that must be included in the annual percentage rate indicated on the form. The form will also include the security offered for the loan—presumably the house itself—and information on prepayment and late-payment charges.

Careful reading of the disclosure form can provide answers to most of the key questions governing your relationship with the lending institution. Here's one case where disclosure exists; it's up to the borrower to study the information carefully.

In June 1975, the Real Estate Settlement Procedures Act (RESPA) went into effect. Designed to help home buyers shop around, RESPA required that the lender make a "good faith" estimate of closing costs, to be followed by full disclosure 24 hours before closing. At the mortgage interview, the applicant must be given a booklet called "How to Buy a Home." The law also bans referral fees for the lender's help in lining up insurance or other services. Originally loaded with complex reporting requirements which could cause excessive delays, RESPA was simplified soon after it went into effect. The law now helps consumers shop for mortgages.

"Points" are a not-too-hidden device for increasing the interest payment. This device is like a balloon-in-reverse, because the special lump-sum interest payment comes at the start of the loan. Points go by a variety of names but can generally be found on the disclosure statement as a fee payable to the bank for its trouble in making the loan. The term itself refers to a percentage of the amount of the loan itself. A single point refers to 1 percent of the loan amount. Thus, on an 8-percent loan, one point pushes the interest for the first year to 9 percent. Banks and thrifts have no statutory right to charge points. Their presence usually reflects competitive conditions in the local market. The purchaser should try to bargain on points as much as market conditions permit.

Frequently, banks and thrifts charge prepayment penalties. With the mortgage running for 25 or 30 years, the possibility that you will pay it off in advance is relatively high. So is the amount of the penalty. It may be as much as six months' interest or a percentage of the balance due on the principal—in effect, more points.

Like points, prepayment charges may be negotiable. The bank or thrift may give up the right to make such a charge if the borrower is selling another house to a person who will continue to mortgage it at the same institution. That way, the lender keeps the old house on the books and adds one. In fact, perhaps neither purchaser will have to accept a prepayment penalty. Obviously, banks may waive the prepayment penalty at the time of repayment if prevailing interest rates at that time are higher than the rate on the existing mortgage. The bank or thrift wants to dispose of lower-rate mortgages when it can. Finally, good customers of the bank or thrift are generally in a sound position to negotiate on this point. It's important to bargain about the prepayment penalty at the time the mortgage loan is made, and then, if it has been included in the terms, at the time of prepayment itself. While the penalty supposedly indemnifies the bank for a prepayment that may disturb their financial planning, from the borrower's viewpoint there is no reason why any penalty should be due for simply exceeding the requirements of the loan agreement.

Some mortgages contain clauses stating that they are "due on encumbrance," which means that if the property is pledged as security on any other loan, including a second mortgage, the first mortgage is immediately due in full. While this is not legal in some places and usually not enforced when it is legal, the purchaser should watch for it and request that it be deleted. In general, banks and thrifts are wary about any encumbrances that might be on a piece of property before the loan is made, but their priority of interest is usually reassuring enough to allow them to maintain the loan even if a second mortgage is taken later.

Mortgages frequently contain "due-on-sale" clauses. The loan must be paid in full when the property is sold. While the bank may extend the mortgage to the new owner, it is not obligated to do so. In addition, the prepayment penalty may be levied. San Francisco Consumer Action reports that this provision is being tested in court.

If the borrower fails to make the regular mortgage payment within a certain allowed period beyond the due date, he or she will probably have to pay a late charge. The charge may be levied either on the payment itself—perhaps as much as 4 percent—or it may be calculated on the basis of the entire outstanding balance. The California Supreme Court has ruled against a late penalty based on the entire balance, since it is entirely unrelated to the damage to the bank resulting from late payment. But the late penalty itself is perfectly legal.

Beyond the security of the house itself, the bank may seek additional backing for the loan. The disclosure statement will indicate such added security, which may include property later added to the mortgaged premises and any deposits the borrower has with the lending institution. Recourse to such deposits is the offset and may discourage the borrower from leaving significant sums in the lending institution. In any case, given rising real-estate prices, the borrower should not need to put up additional collateral and should not provide the bank with such security.

Above all, watch out for "the escrow screw." The bank or thrift and, in the case of FHA loans, must, require that the regular mortgage payments also include a prorated share of local taxes and insurance premiums. This money is not paid out as soon as it is received. The bank keeps it in "escrow" or in an "impound" account. Because property taxes may be due only once or twice a year and insurance can be paid by annual premiums, the regular monthly payments amount to forced savings.

The logic behind the escrow payments is obvious. The lender does not want to see the house attached for failure to pay taxes or lost through fire because it was uninsured. Of course, the bank or thrift can easily determine if taxes are paid and require proof of continuous insurance without actually handling the payment themselves. Only for those people who will find it difficult to save the funds for the required payment is the escrow account an advantage.

In almost all cases, lenders refuse to pay interest on escrow accounts, although they themselves are earning interest on them. The California bank survey calculated that the borrower may lose over $750 on a 30-year loan, using a 5-percent interest rate, when the amount in escrow averages $500 a year.

Along with the recent trend to require interest payments on security deposits with telephone and other utility companies, efforts are being made to require payment of interest on escrow accounts. In New York, Massachusetts, Connecticut, Maryland, and a growing number of states, the law requires the payment of interest on escrow accounts.

Borrowers can insist that they do not want an escrow account, except where the FHA leaves them no choice. In fact, all property tax payers should be opposed to the money's being held in escrow instead of going directly to the local government. As matters stand now, the bank holds the escrow money until the date it is due. In the meantime, the localities must make tax-anticipation loans, perhaps from the selfsame banks. Because local expenditures continue all year, the towns and cities borrow funds to operate until the bank turns over to them the funds in escrow accounts. The interest costs paid by the local governments are, of course, passed on to the property owners in that locality. Thus, the escrow system not only denies them interest but actually forces them to share in the interest paid to the bank by the local government. Yet those who favor escrow accounts say that local governments are the chief beneficiaries because their collection costs are held down.

Some institutions offer alternatives to escrow. Under the capitalization method, monthly tax and insurance payments are credited against the outstanding mortgage principal until they must be paid to the local government or insurance company. As a result, the amount of mortgage interest is lowered. In effect, the thrift using the capitalization method is paying interest on the escrow funds.

Other savings institutions waive escrow if the purchaser opens an interest-bearing savings account in the amount of the annual tax bill. While the principal cannot be withdrawn from the account even to pay taxes, the interest is available.

Still another alternative provides for giving the purchaser the option of closing out the escrow account when his or her equity in the property reaches 40 percent. At that point, the bank figures, equity interest will be a powerful incentive to the borrower to keep up tax payments.

Redlining

Some prospective homeowners have found that they simply cannot obtain a mortgage because the house they want to buy is located in the wrong part of town. Banks rule out entire neighborhoods on the grounds their future prospects are either marginal or poor. They believe that even solid citizens may want to get rid of their homes at a later date and won't be able to find buyers. As a result, the banks would be stuck with defaulted mortgage loans.

This system of ruling certain areas off the mortgage map is called "redlining." Bankers object to the use of the term in a negative sense, but they admit that such a practice seems eminently sensible to them. In New York, savings banks made a deal with political leaders that would permit them to offer checking accounts in return for their agreement to commit 15 percent of their investments to a statewide pool for redlined areas. The banks accepted this formula on the condition that the funds be distributed by the pool, thus insulating individual banks from local pressure to make high-risk mortgage loans. Ultimately, the deal fell through, because of opposition from commercial banks.

Without either such incentives or direct government financial intervention in the form of housing subsidies or loan guarantees, redlining can be expected to continue. As a result, it can perpetuate the decay of neighborhoods, because it would deny loans to those very middle-class people whose presence could help begin the reconstruction of an area.

The Home Mortgage Disclosure Act requires disclosure of where banks make mortgage loans by zip code area. That probably won't end redlining, but it may discourage banks that wanted to avoid the image of being the cause of slums.

The Moment of Truth

The closing for the purchase of a house always involves a certain amount of emotion—a combination of anticipation and concern.

While the mortgage loan is only a part of the arrangement required to purchase the new house, it is an essential element in making the deal possible. Thus, the borrower should be as careful as possible in settling on a mortgage.

1. Get a lawyer's help. This is one matter in which the assistance and counsel of a lawyer is invaluable. Find a lawyer who handles a great many mortgage transactions and knows what pitfalls to look for. Shop around for a good lawyer who makes reasonable charges. There's a lot of paperwork and filing of legal documents, all of which can be handled far more efficiently by a lawyer than by yourself.

2. Figure out in advance what you want in the way of a mortgage. You may not be able to obtain every detail you want, but it's desirable to begin negotiating with your interests firmly in mind. The lender certainly looks out for its own best interest. Most important, you should determine how much you can afford in the way of monthly payments. The 20-percent rule is a sound one. If you want to spend more than 25 percent of your gross after-tax income, you may find it hard to get a bank or thrift to lend you the money.

3. Determine your eligibility for an FHA or VA loan. If the house has already been under such an arrangement and you also qualify, the bank or thrift is likely to extend the mortgage with such a guarantee. Remember that you can take steps to determine your own eligibility for a VA loan without waiting for the moment of truth with the bank.

4. Shop around among institutions and ask for Truth-in-Lending and RESPA disclosure forms from those from which you might obtain the mortgage. Go first to those institutions where you have an established relationship, particularly when money is "tight." Remember that home mortgages are the principal business of savings and loans and savings banks.

5. Investigate the various kinds of mortgage plans to determine which might best suit your special needs. Negotiate with the lender on the type of plan.

6. Remember that the longer you take to pay off the mortgage, the more it will cost in interest.

7. Unless you have to buy right away, or mortgage market conditions are particularly favorable, don't buy when

interest rates are at their peak. A small increment in the interest rate can cost thousands of dollars over the years. A few more months' rent is a far smaller price to pay.

8. Be prepared to negotiate with the lender about special terms of the mortgage agreement. Try to avoid paying "points." Ask for the deletion of prepayment penalties and "due-on-encumbrance" or "due-on-sale" clauses. Above all, seek the elimination of the escrow clause. If that fails, ask for interest on the funds you are to pay the bank. Any condition that may seem minor when you sign the mortgage contract may end up costing you a lot of money during the life of the mortgage.

7 Do You Trust Your Bank?

Ask a banker how his trust department is operated and he will, without blinking, cite the dictum of Justice Benjamin Cardozo in *Meinhard* v. *Salmon:* "A trustee is held to something stricter than the morals of the marketplace. Not honesty alone, but the punctilio of an honor most sensitive, is thus the standard of behavior." But he may well be thinking more in terms of Oliver Wendell Holmes's blunt homily in *The Autocrat of the Breakfast Table:* "Put not your trust in money, but put your money in trust."

To many people, the trust department is reserved for rich folks and of little interest to the rest of us. Yet, millions of people are beneficiaries of trusts operated by banks and are completely ignorant of that fact. They are participants in pension funds whose assets are managed by trust departments of commercial banks.

Of course, many large personal trusts have been established by wealthy people who have demonstrated their ability to watch out for their own financial interests. The same cannot be said for their beneficiaries, who, though they may be wealthy, are generally at the mercy of the bank that is trustee. Merely by being wealthy, such people are not deprived of the need for adequate protection as consumers of banks' services.

Trusts are created for a number of reasons. Although you can't take it with you, a trust allows you a measure of control over the wealth you leave behind. The trustee is bound to follow the instructions laid down by the creator of the trust. Trusts may be established not only as a way of handling what the deceased leaves behind; living trusts may be created by people too busy to handle all the details of their own affairs. Employers may ask banks to handle trust funds that are used to provide pensions to employees.

Trusts created by individuals are often designed to lessen Federal taxation on estates. It is possible to delay the imposition of such taxes for several generations through the judicious use of trusts.

A person setting up a trust is free to name anybody as trustee. Banks regard individuals as their greatest competitors for the trust business, because people are likely to name their friends or lawyers to handle their trusts. Banks hustle hard to attract that business. Some 3,804 commercial banks have trust departments. In fact, the names of many large banks reflect the importance of the trust business both in the past and now: Bankers Trust, First Pennsylvania Banking and Trust, Cleveland Trust, Irving Trust. There are only thirty-nine trust companies that are not associated with banks.

The trust business carried on by banks is not just big, it is enormous. At the end of 1971, the assets of commercial bank trust departments represented 22 percent of the assets of all institutional investors in the United States. These trust-fund assets were greater than the assets of all insurance companies and all mutual funds. They now amount to more than $400 billiion.

According to the staff of the House Banking and Currency Committee, "Banks control the management of over 70 percent of all pension fund management, and it has been estimated that by 1980 total assets of pension funds will reach $285 billion."

Institutional investor trading on the New York Stock Exchange has grown to 68 percent of the dollar volume of shares traded, and trading by commercial bank trust departments account for half of it all.

The trust business is dominated by a handful of New York banks. Five banks control about one-fourth of all trust assets: Morgan Guaranty Trust Company, Bankers Trust Company, Chase Manhattan Bank, Citibank and the United States Trust Company. Only 1.8 percent of all banks with trust departments have 72.3 percent of all trust assets. Because you are most likely to be dealing with a big trust bank, we'll take a closer look at them. In smaller banks, you may find that you get more personal service and there is probably less chance for abuse of trust.

Trust departments have a variety of customers, depending on the type of account. The most typical of all trust accounts is the personal trust. By a living trust, a living person transfers assets to the bank to administer in line with a specific agreement. The person can usually terminate the trust. A testamentary trust is created by the will of the deceased. The bank may be trustee on its own or with an individual. It makes decisions, in line with the instructions of the deceased, if any, on how the funds will be invested.

A will may also name a trust department as executor or administrator of an estate. The bank will then take on a variety of tasks in connection with settling the estate and paying taxes.

An employer can hire a trust department to handle an employee benefit trust, most often a pension trust. In theory, the creation of such a trust is an act of generosity by the employer. As a result, the employer has full discretion over how the funds are managed. Occasionally, the company shares control with its employees in recognition of their having earned at least a part of the funds in the pension trust.

Finally, a person who is a trustee may hire a bank as his or her agent. With an agency account, the trust department may be required to consult the trustee before making any investment decision. If not, there's not much practical difference between being an agent and being trustee.

Aside from those who create trusts, the beneficiaries must also be regarded as customers of the bank. They fall into two general categories: members of the family and close friends in the case of personal, estate, and some agency accounts, or employees in the case of employee benefit and other agency accounts.

What the banks do with the funds placed at their disposal can determine the standard of living and the kind of retirement of a great number of people. In 1972, there were

1,218,236 separate trust accounts.

Obviously, trust departments, taken together, have a lot of clout. What they do can have a major impact on the national economy, and that, in turn, comes home to virtually everybody.

The Giant

With the enormous assets under their control, the trust departments can obviously purchase large blocks of stock in major American corporations. This potential power is accentuated by the policy of most trust departments not to overdiversify. Stock purchases can usually be made only from a limited list, and the trust departments tend to follow the conventional wisdom. They, and not the beneficiaries, vote the shares they hold, thus giving them a powerful tool to influence corporate policy. The control of stockholders over the affairs of the corporations has clearly become meaningless, especially as the number of shareholders has increased. Now, corporation management may be under the control of the banks.

A Twentieth Century Fund report on commercial bank trust departments, based on a survey of about seventy such departments, found, in fact, that such control is rarely exercised. Instead, the trust departments tend either to support management's own decisions or to dispose of the stock they hold. Nonetheless, occasions such as planned corporate mergers and acquisitions arise where the trust departments can have a great influence on management's decisions.

The extent of the possible leverage that can be exercised by the trust departments is even greater than might appear by their sheer size. The commercial side of the bank may make loans to a corporation. It obviously has an interest in seeing that firm succeed and be able to repay that loan. How it performs in the stock market is one indicator of how well a firm is doing. When the bank's trust department buys stock in that corporation, the price of the stock rises. Or if a corporation leaves major deposits with the commercial side of the bank, it may get its reward in terms of purchases of its stock made by the trust department.

The Twentieth Century Fund report found that "in many cases" trust departments obtained corporate customers as part of a reciprocal business relationship that "may lend itself to a subtle form of coercion. Business customers may simply be afraid of" displeasing a powerful creditor. So they come partially under a bank's control by giving up their discretion about who will manage their funds when they place those funds in a trust department, not by choice but under pressure.

Perhaps the most obvious way in which a link is established between the commercial concerns of the bank and the trust department is through interlocking directorships. For example, seven of the directors of the Penn Central Transportation Company were also directors of the banks whose trust departments held major blocks of Penn Central stock and whose commercial departments were prepared to lend the ailing railroad $225 million if they received a government guarantee (which they did not get). Simply because banks tend to choose captains of industry to serve on their boards of directors, it is virtually inevitable that the distinctions between the banks and the corporations will blur. In short, banks can easily get around ethical prohibitions on mingling commercial department and trust department activities.

Bank trust departments are the single most important kind of institutional investor. In fact, it may even be inaccurate to consider them investors rather than traders, because they are in and out of the market so frequently. Their trading represents about 34 percent of the dollar volume of all shares traded on the New York Stock Exchange and is probably also of great significance in other exchanges and even the over-the-counter market.

Trust departments depend to a great extent on other people's research, and they tend to go with the crowd. As a result, the investments are not highly speculative, but they do represent a major influence on those very companies that are considēd the bellwethers of the economy.

When prices of these stocks begin to climb, the trust departments hurry into the market to buy, not wanting to miss a good thing. As a result, they drive the prices up even further. Exactly the reverse takes place in a falling market. Clearly, this pattern of buying and selling disrupts the market and penalizes the smaller investor, who inevitably will be further behind the trend than the banks. Because bank boards are liberally sprinkled with top executives of the firms whose stock is being traded, many fear that the right word here and there enables the banks to act with considerable speed in the light of changing market conditions. This would be illegal and has not been proved.

Which firms? These are the ten largest common-stock holdings of First National City Bank in 1971: IBM, Xerox, Eastman Kodak, Avon, Coca-Cola, GM, Merck, Sears, GE, and 3M. The make-up of the biggest holdings in the overall portfolio of Citibank and others obviously doesn't change much from year to year. What's more, trust fund money is heavily concentrated in the few leading stocks. In 1972, one-third of Manufacturers Hanover's portfolio consisted of just ten stocks.

In short, for the average investor, who is likely to buy some of the same stocks as the trust departments, a part of his or her wealth is, in effect, under the direct and considerable influence of those departments.

Personal Trusts, or the Hand Is Quicker Than the Eye

To paraphrase Winston Churchill, a trust department is a myth shrouded in a haze covered by obfuscation. Of all the aspects of banking activity, the banks are less willing to talk about their trust departments than about any other aspect of their operations. The only study of how these departments actually operate was carried out by Nader's Raiders in their study of Citibank. They built up information by searching out and questioning beneficiaries of trusts managed by Citibank. Many of them were afraid to talk with the investigators because they felt themselves totally at the mercy of the trust officers.

Often, those who establish trusts to be handled by banks don't know what they are getting themselves into. Initially, their lawyers draw up the trust agreements, and they often suggest that the settlor, as the person creating the trust is called, turn over management to a bank. Some lawyers steer business toward banks because they are virtually guaranteed that the banks will turn around and hire them as counsel for the estate or trust. If an individual is named trustee, he may choose his own lawyer to carry out that job.

For a number of reasons, this is one time when following a lawyer's advice may amount to a costly mistake. While a relative or friend may not accept an executor's fee, the bank will insist on the amount the law allows and probably more. What's more, some lawyers will simply accept the standard trust form prepared by the bank and pass it on to their clients. The trouble with the standard form is that it gives the bank complete discretion over the funds placed in trust. That means that the bank can even invest in its own stock and, of course, exercise the voting rights. Such a policy raises the question of whether the settlor's wishes are being followed and whether such a trust really is in the best interest of the beneficiaries.

Most advertising for trust departments boils down to arguments in favor of the simple idea of setting up a trust. A series of brochures prepared by Kennedy Sinclaire, a marketing research firm, for distribution by banks hints at the services of the trust department. But their appeal is summarized as a combination of convenience ("Gain more time and peace of mind. Put us in charge of your investments"), expertise ("Investing on your own in today's market? Then it's you against the professionals"), and personal service ("We're professionals too—but we invest to meet individual needs").

There's a gap between what trust departments promise and what they produce.

The Nader study relates the story of a Mrs. R., a trust

beneficiary who was suddenly informed that the principal in the trust had been shifted predominantly into growth stocks. At seventy-four, she was a good deal more interested in income, and complained that the bank was required to consult her on changes in the portfolio in advance, not simply inform her after the fact. Citibank apologized and said it might do something to rectify the error. "However, as sole trustees charged with the legal responsibility of managing the trust, we cannot honor your request that the entire program be reversed [i.e., put back the way it was before the bank made the change]." By the time the bank got the matter straightened out, the trust had lost over $13,000.

This case says little for the personal service that trust departments claim to provide. But even more important, it did little to contribute to Mrs. R.'s peace of mind. The major problem is the untrammeled nature of the rights that trust departments hold. The deceased are hardly in a position to complain, and the beneficiaries can complain all they want for all the good it will do them.

Trust departments usually receive a portfolio of investments. They almost never leave them unchanged. As indicated earlier, they may convert some of the assets into holdings of the bank's own stock or that of its holding company. Usually, they will liquidate all or part of the portfolio in order to invest the funds in the banks' own common trust funds. These are the same as mutual funds, but are operated by the bank and with the bank's own trusts as customers. Like mutual funds, the common trust funds permit diversification, and a bank may have several of them, each tailored to a specific need; growth, income, or tax-exempt. The bank will give particular importance to the investment performance of these funds. To that extent, a trust with money invested in a common trust fund is actually getting more attention than if it were handled separately, simply because of the limited number of management personnel available to look after trusts.

Acting on behalf of a client, a Boston lawyer once visited a bank and asked to see the holdings of a trust account. He expected to see the actual shares of the corporations in which the trust had invested. Instead, he was handed a computer printout. Gone are the days when banks maintained separate portfolios, supposedly tailored to the specific instructions of the settlor and the specific needs of the beneficiaries.

The desire of the trust department to realize the economies resulting from lumping trusts together is nowhere more evident than when the trust includes shares of a small family-owned company. Holding on to such shares will mean more work, for the bank may have to become involved in the affairs of the firm. Whenever they can, banks liquidate these holdings, often to place the money in common trust funds. The family business may suffer from the rapid disposal of a large block of its outstanding shares, and other members of the family, including some of the trust's beneficiaries, will lose income.

Perhaps all of the activity in a trust account may consist of no more than liquidating holdings and placing the money in a common trust fund. A study by the Securities and Exchange Commission revealed that in 1969, 44 percent of the personal trust accounts they examined had no activity whatsoever. Many of these appear to be small trusts where it may not be worth the bank's efforts because of relatively small fees. The result for the ignored funds is that increasing sums turn out to be held in noninterest-bearing accounts. This cash buildup, if it gets too far out of hand before somebody blows the whistle, can be an indication of inept management. But trust departments are seldom relieved of their trust accounts on the grounds of mismanagement.

Some beneficiaries would probably be happier with inactivity than they are with investment in a common trust fund. When the original portfolio holdings are liquidated prior to putting the money in a common trust, a capital gains tax is due. It's due again when the trust is distributed, because there's no way to hand out stock to the designated recipients. The trust account's share of the common trust fund must be converted to cash and tax paid before the holdings can be distributed.

Acting as sole trustees, banks can play down beneficiaries' interests in favor of playing up to their commercial customers. When trust departments find closely held companies—those owned by just a few people—in their trust accounts, they will often dispose of them. Unfortunately, the banks may well not get the best price, which would best suit the beneficiaries. Instead, they may sell to a purchaser who is a "friend of the bank." In addition, they may invest trust fund assets in "private placements"—shares sold directly by the issuing company rather than through the stock exchange. In this way, the banks can use investments by the trust department instead of loans by the commercial department to extend credit to the customer. The return on such investments is often lower than could be obtained from stocks that are traded on the market. The Twentieth Century Fund reports cites the case of the Mellon Bank, which made heavy private placements of the assets of the Pennsylvania Public School Employees' Retirement Fund and did not produce the income it should have—over an eleven-year period. Customers may actually force trust departments to invest in their shares as a condition of leaving funds on deposit in the commercial department. In none of these cases would the bank place the beneficiaries' interest above those of the commercial customer.

Continental Illinois National Bank reports that its trust department has its large stockholdings in some fifty companies, 75 percent of which borrow money commercially from the bank and 37 percent of which have outstanding credit of more than $5 million each. This information does not prove that the bank places the customer ahead of the beneficiary, but the opportunity exists. In 1973, the Air Line Pilots Association sued Continental on the grounds that it had held on to weak stocks simply because they were issued by companies to which the bank had lent money. In one case, in which a stock fell to 7 percent of its initial value over a six-year period, Continental was the principal creditor of the issuing corporation.

Yet another way that banks can harm beneficiaries in order to help commercial customers stems from the banks' desire to support management. They will vote proxies in favor of management positions even if beneficiaries lose. In one case, a trust department opposed a proposed corporate rule that would have reduced its voting power and hence harmed the beneficiaries. But it was forced to acquiesce in the new rule by the commercial department. The trust department could not have sold its shares in the corporation because its holdings were so large that merely starting such a sale would have sharply reduced the value of shares not yet sold.

It might appear that many of the problems resulting from the complete freedom of action given banks under trusts that they manage alone could be eliminated by the creation of co-trusts. In such cases, the trust department would be obliged to share the decision-making on investment. This course is almost certain to be more costly, because the trust will have to pay both trustees. Usually the bank will not cut its fee, even if it has a share of authority. Citibank makes no bones about its desire to call the shots even when there's a co-trustee. Said one unfortunate person who found himself in an uneven partnership with the bank: "The bank likes to act on its own even if you are a co-trustee. They don't accept suggestions on investments other than their own. Many times I've suggested good income stocks, but they wouldn't go along, so I finally had to accept their choices."

Perhaps the most appealing reason for installing a bank as trustee is the virtual certainty that it will go on operating even after close family and friends are no longer around. As a trust reaches across the years, the bank is expected to be the one constant and reliable feature.

But the bank is people, especially as far as the beneficiaries are concerned. Those trust department brochures say: "In effect, our entire investment staff will be placed at your family's disposal." In fact, with all the different faces they will see, it may actually seem as though they are served by the entire staff—one after another. As one beneficiary in the Nader study of Citibank wrote: "They change trust officers so often, one can never count on talking to the same man from year to year."

According to the Nader study findings, the trust department is far from the most desirable place to work in the bank from the employees' viewpoint. At Citibank there are sixty portfolio managers for 10,000 personal trust accounts. That works out to 160 accounts for each manager. No wonder they complain of being frustrated and underpaid. The chances for advancement are not considered attractive because there are only limited opportunities within the department. The Twentieth Century Fund report found: "In the larger trust banks, personal trust portfolio managers have had relatively low status."

The general atmosphere is reflected in the poor service at Citibank, about which customers complain. Checks arrive six months late, tax information is inadequate, and funds lay idle, not earning interest. Occasionally, securities can be misplaced or lost.

In short, personal trusts are not personal. The recipient of income from one may feel more like a victim than a beneficiary.

Pensions: You Bet Your Life

More than thirty million people participate in pension funds. Everybody contributes to them indirectly through tax laws that favor their creation. Commercial bank trust departments handle the great majority of these pension funds. Pension trust funds are big business and, as with personal trusts, the ultimate beneficiaries often seem to be given little consideration by the bank.

Employers generally determine what they want or plan to accomplish in terms of benefit level and have an actuary determine the funds needed to accomplish this goal. They then turn to the trust department to manage the pension fund. An agreement is signed between the employer and the bank. In relatively few cases do the workers themselves have a voice in the agreement. Then, worker representatives sit on the board of the pension fund. But most employers regard their contributions to a pension fund as entirely their own money. They do not see it as money that would otherwise have been paid to the workers in the form of wages. As a result, the workers have no right to examine the trustee's work, except when it may be too late.

A pension fund is similar to a living trust in that the settlor in the form of the employer remains on the scene. Does that mean that the bank, even though it is the trustee, is relieved of certain responsibilities? For example, if the money placed in the fund is inadequate to provide the promised benefit level, is it up to the bank to say so, or can it remain silent and hope that the employer will inform the workers in time? If the bank is relieved of this responsibility, it has been relieved of one of the basic obligations of trusteeship—accountability to the beneficiary.

The pension reform law that was enacted in 1974 was designed to eliminate abuses that resulted from the employer's having too great a control over the funds placed in a pension or profit-sharing plan. The management could divert the funds out of the plan, leaving inadequate money in the till and causing people who retired to lose the pensions they had earned over a period of years. Although not so directly as the employers themselves, the trust departments had participated in actions that had the same result.

The bank is in the best position to know if the amount the employer says he is putting in the pension fund is actually being deposited. If the bank remains silent, it could become as implicated as the employer in the failure to pay out adequate benefits later.

Sometimes firms would open pension trust accounts at certain banks in the belief or on the understanding that the bank would invest a portion of those funds in those firms. This is called self-dealing. While perhaps no more than 5 percent of the fund might be invested in the employer's company or its affiliate, if that company went broke, its own employees were unduly penalized. Studies indicate that self-dealing in profit-sharing plans may be as high as 80 percent of the stock in the pension fund.

Obviously, just how well trust departments do when they invest the pension funds determines how adequately pensions will be financed and the amount of resources employers will have to draw from other purposes in order to feed the fund. Often those funds will come out of planned pay raises, so the workers will have to accept less satisfactory contracts because the trust departments have not done as well as they should have.

Performance studies indicate that the employee benefit funds were not able to outperform the market during a period when stock prices were rising steadily. In other words, the trust department managers did no better than an investor would have done, investing in the stocks included in Standard & Poor's 500 index. Almost half the bank-managed employee benefit funds did not do so well as the market as a whole. The Nader group looked at Citibank's nine common trust funds for pensions and found that "in seven of the nine funds employers during this period [1968–71] would have done better had they put their pension funds into savings accounts."

According to a Twentieth Century Fund report on the management of pension fund assets, the trust departments claim that simply keeping up with Standard & Poor's 500 is a prodigious accomplishment. They say that they purchase so much stock that they can only buy shares in the largest companies. Even then, they must proceed carefully in trading the large blocks of stock they own for fear of disrupting the stock market. They envy the small investor who has much greater flexibility to purchase stock issues in smaller companies that undergo periods of rapid growth. The trust departments fail to mention that they have access to the kind of research about potential stock investments or sales that is unavailable to the smaller investor. He or she may find out about a change in the fortunes of a company only after the trust departments have already acted to buy or sell as a result of their better access to information.

Misplaced Trust

Trust departments have been under pressure from the House Ways and Means Committee, the SEC, and increasingly from the press to eliminate a number of practices that appear to undermine their ability to operate according to "the punctilio of an honor the most sensitive." In fact, most of the reformers would even accept a close approximation, because the list of problem areas is so long.

Trust departments must conduct their stock transactions through stockbrokers. Banks can send their business through those brokers who keep their accounts in the commercial department, increasing their business with a given brokerage firm as the balance in its account increases. The trust department can increase account activity as a way of increasing broker commissions. The broker then puts his increased profits in the bank. In that way, the bank can bleed a pension fund, which pays the brokerage fees, for its own profit. In addition, it may carry out transactions through brokerage firms when it could conduct trades where their services were not required. Finally, banks can choose brokers, not on the basis of their ability, but because they have accounts in the bank. All of this can cost beneficiaries money. And it is illegal, simply because a trustee is not supposed to profit from a trust. In September 1973, Jeffrey M. Bucher, a member of the Board of Governors of the Federal Reserve System, could report: "The mere threat of Justice Department action, along with some journalistic criticism of the practice, has led to the voluntary elimination of 'tie-in' practices of this type by most institutions." Obviously, banks got pretty public-spirited under the "mere threat" of Federal prosecution.

Trust departments can, as we have seen, allow cash balances to build up without such funds earning any income. Such cash results from the receipt of dividend payments or employer contributions to pension plans. The banks can lend this cash, usually to themselves, at no interest. The Twentieth Century Fund report on commercial bank trust departments found that "for the large banks, between about 50 per cent and over 90 per cent of all in-bank trust deposits seem to be classified as non-interest bearing. . . ." The Federal Reserve Bank of New York found that in 1971 ten New York banks made a profit of $114 million as a result of using these cash balances to make loans. This profit ensured that the trust departments would do more than break even on their operations. Almost all of this money should, under the law governing trusts, have gone to the beneficiaries of trust accounts.

Purchases of stocks in firms having a commercial relationship with the bank can also drive down income. For example, the pension fund of Bakery Drivers Local 816 sued Bankers Trust for funneling trust money into unwise and low-return investments and loans to the bank's commercial clients. As a result, the annual return on the fund was 0.7 percent, while similar funds were receiving between 6 and 10 percent. Of course, a trust department can also fail to sell when it does not want to depress the stock of a commercial client, whatever the effect on beneficiaries. Finally, as mentioned earlier, the bank can obtain for itself authorization to invest in its own stock.

Other abuses can arise if banks discriminate among their trust customers. The banks can buy and sell among accounts. If a favored account has undesirable stocks in its portfolio, the situation can be improved immediately by dumping the "dog" into another trust account. Here is one story recounted in the Twentieth Century Fund report on commercial bank trust departments:

> One customer, highly dependent on credit from a powerful trust institution, was virtually forced to place its pension fund with the bank. Approximately 10 per cent of the assets of this fund were shortly thereafter placed in the stock of a financially stricken customer with whom the bank was deeply involved and whose stock was of less than investment grade. Almost immediately after acquisition, this issue fell to a small fraction of its original price. The investment banker (who told this story) believes that a very strong and alert pension fund customer of the bank learned of the coming debacle and insisted that the shares of the sagging company be removed from its portfolio. Because the market was thin, the shares were placed in weaker portfolios. The investment banker claims that the customer knew this but was too dependent on bank credit to withdraw, sue or even complain.

Many of these practices that cost beneficiaries money result from the obvious overlapping of trust and commercial functions, which are, theoretically at least, barred by law. But this overlap has been the cause of the most serious charges against banks.

The trust department of Denver U.S. National Bank sold *Denver Post* stock to Helen Bonfils, a member of a family with which the bank had maintained long and profitable commercial arrangements. It turned down a better offer from S. I. Newhouse, who had no ties to the bank. Incidentally, the beneficiaries lost about $2.7 million because the sale went to Bonfils, until the court ordered the bank to pay that much to the trusts. Martin Mayer, in *The Bankers,* has been critical of the court, Nader, and the House Banking and Currency Committee for supporting this punitive action. "There are few causes on which men of goodwill would more quickly agree," he says, "than the desirability of keeping local newspapers locally-owned wherever possible." There's at least the possibility that the beneficiaries of trust accounts managed by Denver U.S. National might have disagreed, and "men of goodwill" sometimes have sympathy for widows and orphans.

Most of the practices have brought on lawsuits. As a result, banks have taken steps to reform for fear of continued pressure in the courts. But there's still room for change.

The Road Back toward Trust

One study group after another has recommended major changes in the operation of trust departments. These prescriptions for purity come mostly as a result of the abuses having reached a point where pressure from beneficiaries could no longer be ignored.

The Presidential Commission on Financial Structure and Regulation, known as the Hunt Commission, has suggested that a wall be built between trust and commercial departments in banks with trust assets greater than $200 million. Just why smaller trust departments were not included is not clear. The Hunt Commission also asked for rules banning the purchase or sale of securities on the basis of inside information. "At the present time," it said, "if bank trust officers have inside information they are in a dilemma. If they use it in a transaction, they may be charged with misconduct. If they have information and do not apply it, they may be charged with not doing the best they can for their clients. A clear rule on correct behavior should be enunciated."

The staff of the House Banking and Currency Committee went much further. It called for the complete separation of trust and commercial departments in banks where the total trust assets exceed $200 million. A Federal Trust Management Commission was recommended to regulate the management of certain funds, including pension plans.

Whether the ultimate barrier be a wall or complete separation, with the new trust company part of the same holding company as the bank, the critical issue will be how much information is communicated back and forth. The regulators will have to do a better job monitoring such exchanges.

There is no doubt that the trust departments could make it on their own. While banks wail that trust departments lose money, very few are closed down. The independent trust companies, those few not linked with banks, seem to be able to operate, although some critics claim they can do so only because they charge higher fees than the trust departments. They may also provide better and more personalized service.

Looking Out for Number One

These reforms will not come overnight and there is no assurance that they will work. In the meantime, millions of persons may continue to find themselves at the mercy of trust departments. The Nader study and this survey of trust operations lead to the recommendation of steps individuals and institutions should take to protect their own interests.

1. Lawyers should be required under standard practices of the bar to disclose to their clients all of the possible advantages and disadvantages of a trust agreement and their own present and potential relationship with the bank. All of this should be in writing. A client can, at any time, request such a statement from his or her lawyer.

2. Banks should be banned from advertising that they provide personalized or individual services unless they actually do. It may be satisfactory for some settlors to have their trust funds lumped with others for investment purposes, and they certainly have the right to know that in advance.

3. Whatever they advertise, banks should pay greater attention to ensuring some continuity of service to beneficiaries.

4. Trust departments should not be allowed to liquidate the assets of a trust fund for the purpose of investing the money in a common trust fund unless they first obtain the consent of the settlor, if possible, or the beneficiaries.

5. Banks acting as trustees for employee benefit funds should assume the responsibility for preventing self-dealing. Trust departments can simply refuse to execute the orders of employers to purchase company stock. If this were the standard for all trust departments, there would be no risk of losing clients to other banks that would execute self-dealing orders.

6. Trust departments should also take upon themselves the responsibility for informing potential beneficiaries of pension plans when the plan is not fully funded. The bank is, after all, maintaining the funds for their benefit, often as a result of a collective-bargaining agreement. It owes the beneficiaries this information. Otherwise, it is aiding in a serious breach of contract.

7. Employees should assert their rights to have a share in the ultimate control of pension funds. The myth that the employer uses his own funds to start a trust fund benefiting his employees has been discredited. The pension reform law of 1974 recognizes the lack of faithful execution by employers of their obligations to employees. Clearly, the Federal government will assume a new enforcement role. But

employees must be certain to protect themselves. This includes seeking specialists other than banks to handle pension funds.

8. Banks should be required to turn over any profits from holding cash to the trust funds. If this change affects their profitability, they should reexamine their rate structure. Perhaps settlors and beneficiaries would be willing to pay a higher price if they felt they were receiving better service.

9. Banks should be required to greatly improve their disclosure practices. People thinking of creating trust accounts should determine which trust departments would be willing to provide them with detailed information about their operations. In particular, the banks should be prepared to indicate the major investments of their common trust funds and major holdings of stock outside the trust funds. In addition, the banks should reveal the performance of the common trust funds. They should disclose interlocking directorates and outstanding loans to companies whose stock is held in the trust departments. All of this information will help those directly involved in a trust account. That is reasonable.

10. Settlors should make clear their wishes about how stock will be voted. Obviously, banks should not be allowed to vote their own stock. But the broader problem relates to social and environmental issues. Many people feel that shares should be voted not only with corporate profits in mind but also with respect to matters ranging from antipollution efforts to accomplishments in bringing women and minorities into positions of responsibility. In 1973, the American Bankers Association adopted Guidelines for Dealing with Corporate Responsibility Issues. These state, in part:

> If as an investment manager the fiduciary believes that a given corporation's activity or inactivity with respect to social or environmental issues is likely substantially to impact the earnings of the corporation or its long-term investment performance, the fiduciary should make an investment decision based upon those investment factors.

In other words, unless what a corporation is doing helps its earnings, sell the stock. It will take a direct order by the settlor to change the orientation.

11. While beneficiaries cannot simply assert new rights for themselves, there seems little doubt that they should have a greater say over the control of the funds on which they may depend. Of course, the basic concept of the trust cannot be defeated. Most are created because the settlor believes that the beneficiaries will not be sufficiently capable of managing the funds to ensure that his or her wishes will be carried out. But beneficiaries should be able to take legal action to have a trustee changed when they become the victims of incompetence or management not in their best interests. In addition, the decision of the beneficiaries about what they wish from the fund ought to be required to be followed by the bank. Thus, the seventy-four-old woman wanting income and not growth stocks should have her way unless it directly violates the wishes of the settlor. If a group of children want income stressed so their widowed mother will have an adequate income rather than growth issues that will ensure a larger inheritance for them, their wishes ought to be followed. Finally, banks should treat beneficiaries as those for whom the trust exists, not merely as victims of trust department decisions, who have no right of protest.

12. Ask how trust officers are compensated. If they receive a salary rather than a commission they may not be so tempted to talk you into using unnecessary bank services.

13. Finally, any person thinking of setting up a trust and turning it over to a bank to manage ought to review that decision carefully. Obviously, as long as the Federal tax laws encourage the creation of trusts, people should use them. But it may be questionable whether a bank can do any better than a settlor who leaves fairly explicit investment instructions with an attorney or other qualified individual. When everything is taken into account, trust funds administered by banks did not do any better than the stock market as a whole during a period of sustained growth in stock values. Certainly, because trust departments like to invest

in common stock, funds have plunged with the market. If a trust fund had been required merely to place funds in a savings account at any time in recent years, it would have provided a better return than did the investment of trust departments. While there is no guarantee that that would always be true, this period includes both a rapidly rising and rapidly falling market. Choosing management by a trust department instead of putting the money into a savings account may simply be a case of overlooking the obvious.

8 The Regulators

At 3:00 P.M. on Thursday, October 18, 1973, about 300 men and women, looking for all the world like conservative bankers, converged on the 63 offices of the United States National Bank of San Diego. Although the bank offices were closing just at that hour, they had no trouble getting past the guard. They worked for the bank's new owner.

As these people moved through the door, 165 men and women, who had formally moved onto the premises just twenty-four hours earlier, began to pack their belongings and make ready to leave. Most of the bank staff just watched the proceedings, although they were listening to orders from their new owner's representatives and answering questions.

At that moment, ownership of the United States National Bank, with assets of $1,265,868,000, had passed from C. Arnholt Smith and his friends to an outfit called the Federal Deposit Insurance Corporation. The 300 were bank examiners and liquidators of the FDIC. The 165 were national bank examiners who work for the Comptroller of the Currency, the man who had just decided to close the bank.

The dramatic event at 3:00 P.M. was the result of careful and clandestine planning. Secrecy was essential to prevent a run on the bank that might result from a sudden loss of confidence.

As we shall see later, the Comptroller, an official of the Treasury Department, had through the reports of his bank examiners come to believe that the USNB no longer had enough cash on hand or the ability to come up with the cash needed to meet expected demand for withdrawals. While bank assets substantially exceeded the amount that depositors had left with USNB, some of those assets were in the form of loans that would probably never be repaid. In any case, they couldn't be repaid when their proceeds were needed. If those people who wanted to make withdrawals could not get their money, panic would spread, and others, who had not planned to touch their deposits, would also seek to get their money out of the USNB. The result would be a run on the bank, which would not have time even to convert its loans into cash to meet depositors' demands.

James E. Smith, the Comptroller of the Currency, knew the time had come to act. That's why on October 17 he had sent his own examiners, who had entered the bank before it closed and had worked through the night and the next day, checking the cash, the loan collateral, and the items kept in safekeeping by the USNB. They had also supervised the bank's closing that day and had monitored its activities all the following day. In that way, the Comptroller could know exactly the condition of the bank when he declared that it was "insolvent"—out of cash. Then the FDIC took over as the bank went into receivership.

But the FDIC was to keep control of the bank for a very short time. At 3:00 P.M. on October 18, just as the FDIC people were taking over USNB, the FDIC itself was putting the bank on the selling block. Within an hour, three bids were received. They were opened, and at 4:30 P.M., the FDIC accepted the high bid of $89.5 million from the Crocker National Bank. Frank Wille, chairman of the FDIC, had his lawyers in San Diego informed of the sale, and they went directly to the U.S. District Court where Judge Leland C. Nielsen, who had been alerted, was standing by. He held an immediate hearing and approved the purchase by Crocker National, which would also assume many of the USNB's obligations. At 6:15 P.M., the deal was final. The next day, all of the USNB's offices opened as branches of the Crocker National Bank. For 335,000 depositors, there was little difference. The 300 men and women of the FDIC packed up their attaché cases and left.

The largest bank failure in the history of the United States until that time (before the collapse of the Franklin National) had taken place and no depositor had lost a cent.

But what of the bad loans? Crocker had assumed all the "clean" assets and liabilities of the USNB. As receiver, the FDIC did not sell some $240 million in questionable assets, mostly related to loans granted those activities of C. Arnholt Smith, the shareholder who had controlled the bank. The FDIC had to turn many of these assets into cash to meet outstanding claims against the bank. But none of these claims comprised deposits, which are insured by the FDIC.

All of this happened because a national bank examiner, together with some colleagues, one day tapped discreetly on the doors of the USNB and said they had come to look at the books. He was operating according to a dry little statement in a dry little booklet called *Bank Supervision.* It reads: "Disclosure . . . is often the result of surprise and this element has an important place in examining techniques." When bank examiners arrive on the scene, they assume actual control of bank operations. Their job is to verify that the bank is operating soundly and safely and within the law. Above all, they represent the depositors and other bank creditors.

But bank examination to prevent bank failure is only a small part of the activities of the regulators.

Who They Are

Bank regulation has grown slowly over the years until there is now a confusing array of supervisory organizations. In the nineteenth century, after a brief flirtation with the First and Second Banks of the United States, through which the Federal government itself got into the banking business, all commercial banks were privately owned and chartered by the states. Actually they were subject to only the loosest supervision by state authorities.

These commercial banks issued currency because there was no truly national currency. When, during the Civil War, it became necessary to raise funds nationally to wage a national war, a law was passed creating such a currency and also providing for the Federal chartering of "national" banks that would also be privately owned. The Comptroller of the Currency was given the power to issue the charters and to supervise these banks.

Throughout the nineteenth century, the notion of "money" meant just that—the national currency. For decades, the debate raged about how much money there ought to be. If gold alone backed the dollar, the growth of the money supply would be limited. If silver were also used as backing, more dollars could be printed. With the increasing industrialization and urbanization of the United States, the need developed to be able to expand and reduce the amount of money by government policy and not by the printing press alone.

In 1913, the Federal Reserve System was created to "furnish an elastic currency." It would act through the national banks, all of which would be members, and through those state banks that wished to become members. Because its interests would be different from those of the Comptroller of the Currency, it was given its own supervisory powers over its members.

After the Great Depression and the collapse of many banks, yet another Federal agency was created, the FDIC. State banks, not Federal Reserve members, were authorized to purchase deposit insurance, which made them subject to Federal regulation for the first time. Because the FDIC has to provide insurance, it was authorized to examine insured banks to make sure that they would not go under and draw on the insurance.

Since 1933, then, there have been three Federal supervisory bodies, plus the state authorities. In order to keep out of each other's way, the Federal agencies have divided the primary responsibilities for supervision of commercial banks, as shown in the accompanying table.

Regulator	*Comp-troller*	*Federal Reserve*	*FDIC*	*State Bank-ing Depts.*
National banks (4,747)	X			
State banks: FR members FDIC-insured (1,029)		X		X
State banks: FDIC-insured not FR members (8,597)			X	X
State banks: not FDIC-insured not FR members (270)				X

X = regulatory authority.

Obviously, most state banks are subject to supervision by both state and Federal agencies. They may work independently of each other or they may carry out their own examinations concurrently or, as in the case of New York, they can carry out a joint examination.

The trio of Federal regulatory agencies can be confusing for the banks themselves, let alone the customer who has a question or a complaint about a bank. Each of the three Federal agencies has its headquarters in Washington. In addition, the Comptroller of the Currency operates through fourteen national bank regions, each headed by a regional national bank examiner. The FDIC has twelve districts, each with a supervising examiner at the top. There are twelve Federal Reserve banks, each with its own district. None of the districts is identical. Thus, for example, if a national bank in Evansville, Indiana—subject to all three Federal regulators—were to contact each, it would have to turn to the regional chief national bank examiner in Cleveland, Ohio, the Federal Reserve Bank of St. Louis, and the FDIC district supervising examiner in Madison, Wisconsin. Of course, the Evansville bank would be likely to know exactly which office to contact on a specific matter. The bank's customers would probably not even be aware of the variety of regulatory bodies, much less know where to reach them.

What Do Examiners Do All Day—and Sometimes All Night?

Bank supervisors at both the state and national level have a wide range of responsibilities related to the operation of banks:

- —chartering and organization of banks;
- —periodic examination and requiring banks to correct unsatisfactory or unsound conditions;
- —review of periodic reports on earnings and expenses;
- —advising banks, on request;
- —approval of changes in banking activities and capital structure;
- —authorization of branches and of trust operations;
- —approval of bank mergers;
- —regulation of bank holding companies;
- —regulation of bank service corporations;
- —issuance and enforcement of regulations pursuant to law;
- —liquidation of banks.

Not all agencies conduct all activities. Not all agencies that have the same responsibilities carry them out in the same way. Not all agencies require the same degree of proof of the same operating standard.

The principal tool of the regulators is bank examination. In fact, most of the officials of national and state regulating agencies are examiners. The chief task of the examiner is appraisal, and not, as many believe, audit. The examiner's job is to determine above all if the bank is competently and honestly managed, so that it will not fail, nor, as a matter of policy, cheat its customers. An examination for this purpose may also entail some auditing. For example, some state examiners will check the bookkeeping on checking and savings accounts and require remedial action if too high a level of error is found. But no regulator checks the math in all checking accounts or the calculation of interest in all savings accounts.

When the examiner knocks at the bank door politely but definitely unexpectedly, he or she wants to check on the bank's assets and liabilities (sometimes even by talking to the bank's creditors), determine if all laws are being obeyed, appraise the qualifications of directors and the competence of officers and some employees, and get a general feel of how the bank is being operated. Banks that differ from the norm get recommendations for remedial action.

Perhaps checking of assets is the most important part of the job. If somebody has absconded with funds, some of the assets will be missing. If the bank has been poorly managed, some assets, probably in the form of bad loans, will be of doubtful value.

The Comptroller of the Currency and his examiners are the principal supervisory agency for about one-third of the banks, those with national charters. Indeed, the Comptroller issues the charter and can remove it. By issuing a charter, the Comptroller automatically admits banks to the Federal Reserve System and FDIC insurance. In addition, he authorizes national banks to carry on trust operations and open branches. He must also approve mergers involving national banks. In the case of a national bank (identified by the word "national" in its name or the letters "NA" [National Association] after the name), the first place a customer with a complaint ought to go is the office of the Regional Administrator of National Banks.

While the Comptroller examines national banks and has the greatest supervisory authority over their activities, the Federal Reserve also has considerable direct powers. For both national banks and state member banks, it determines how much money they must hold in reserves. For all banks of any kind, it approves or disapproves the formation of or acquisition by a bank holding company and regulates all loans secured by stock. And except where an entire state has a waiver, it supervises compliance with the Truth-in-Lending law. For state member banks, it exercises the same powers that the Comptroller has over national banks, including the power to charter them. In the early 1960s, Comptroller James Saxon was free and easy in authorizing new banks and branches and in relaxing regulations, so some banks, including the mighty Chase Manhattan, simply applied for national bank status as a way of escaping the more stringent Federal Reserve control. For a customer to know whether he should address a complaint to the Federal Reserve, he would have to ask the bank if it is a member or turn to the state regulatory agency. About 9 percent of banks are classified as state member banks.

The FDIC authorizes branches and mergers, in addition to examining state-insured nonmember banks—more than half of all banks. While it has no chartering power, its regulations extend to all banks with FDIC insurance, including all those directly supervised by the Federal Reserve and the Comptroller. For example, rules governing advertising are issued by the FDIC.

Finally, each of the states has a banking agency that carries on its own examinations of all state banks and authorizes all branches and mergers involving them, and the assumption of trust powers by them. For the few noninsured, nonmember state banks, the state banking agencies are the sole examining authority. State banking agencies vary in size and expertise. In New York, the Banking Department would be large enough to meet the needs of most independent nations. In Nevada, the Banking Department must worry about only four state-chartered banks.

Even this is not a complete list of regulators. Savings and loan associations may be either state or Federally chartered. State-chartered savings and loans, more than 60 percent of the total, are chartered and supervised either by state banking departments or by special savings and loan departments. Federal savings and loans are chartered and supervised by the Federal Home Loan Bank Board, roughly analogous to the Federal Reserve Board. The Federal Savings and Loan Insurance Corporation performs the same functions as the FDIC. For customers who want to find the proper regulatory agency, most of these thrift institutions have the words "savings and loan" in their name. In some states, other names are used—Massachusetts uses the name "cooperative banks," Louisiana uses "homestead societies," and a few other states call them "building and loan associations." FHLB members all have the word "federal" in their name.

Mutual savings banks are all state banks. About two-thirds of them are insured by the FDIC, with all but one of the others insured by the Massachusetts state insurance system. Just to confuse matters further, about 10 percent of the savings banks are members of the FHLB. For the consumer, the appropriate regulatory agencies to turn to would be the FDIC and the state banking agency.

Credit unions are chartered either by the National Credit Union Administration or by state banking authorities. Federally chartered credit unions (the word "federal" appears in the name) have deposit insurance provided through the NCUA on the same basis as the FDIC. Some states authorize their credit unions to obtain NCUA insurance, and others provide their own mandatory insurance programs. For consumers, the regulatory agencies are either the NCUA or the state banking department.

Of course, even before you've been through the maze of agencies to determine the proper one to which you, as a consumer, should appeal, you may wonder what are proper matters of concern for the regulators. In fact, the answer is anything. Because regulators are interested in determining how well banks are run and because they have the authority to order banks to correct their actions in all phases of their operations, any matter where you feel the bank has dealt unfairly or dishonestly with you is properly brought before a regulator.

The first step is to take a complaint to the bank itself. Frequently errors are made through inadvertence and will be immediately corrected. In other cases, the bank may be testing consumer reaction to its efforts to alter or reduce its services, and the bank will generally back away quickly if the consumer complains. In other cases, the bank may actually be cheating on its contractual agreement with a customer (as in calculating interest in a way not indicated when the account was opened) and may also change course if called on its action. The worst situation, of course, is when the depositor is, for any reason, deprived of his or her funds. In addition to all these cases where your immediate interests are concerned, the regulators would be glad to learn of any information you might have that would help in evaluating the overall management of the bank.

If the bank fails to respond satisfactorily to your complaint or inquiry, you should immediately contact the proper regulatory agency. It's important to explain calmly and systematically the situation and what has happened in your contacts with the bank. Try to remember dates, amounts, and the correct location of the branch. Include the account number or the number on the loan agreement. The regulator should be able to proceed quickly to straighten the matter out. Where both a state and a Federal agency have regulatory authority, try the state banking department first.

Because of the nature of their work, banks constitute one of the few totally regulated industries in the country. Government has provided somebody to help you.

Why Banks Fail

In the years between 1930 and 1933, 9,096 banks failed or were suspended from operations. About four-fifths of the deposit loss was sustained by the depositors themselves. This was one of the most devastating effects of the Great Depression and involved the greatest number of bank closings in the shortest period in American history.

The Great Depression was characterized by a steady reduction in the amount of money. Money had been rapidly "created" through the 1920s by the extensive use of credit. The collapse of credit meant that the amount of money or what would be accepted as money was reduced. Credit depends upon confidence. When confidence withers, so does credit. The shortage of money spelled doom for many banks that had either failed to spread their loan risk sufficiently or had simply made bad loans. When the borrowers defaulted, banks did not have enough money on hand to cover deposits. The banks that failed were the weakest, but even they could not have been expected to foresee the economic collapse that others had not expected.

After the Depression reached its low point, Federal regulatory agencies were created and strengthened with the goal of preventing a similar situation from ever happening again. Among the measures were the creation of deposit insurance and tighter controls on just how much money banks could loan to finance stock purchases. With a steadily expanding economy and with these safeguards, the bank-failure rate fell precipitously. In the worst years of the Depression, 11.3 percent of the banks had been closed. In the 1958–71 period, only 0.3 percent suffered a similar fate.

About two-thirds of recent bank failures were due to outright fraud and absconding with funds by bank officers. There is little chance for examiners to prevent such cases unless they stay on the bank's premises at all times. Most of the rest of the closings resulted from banks soliciting deposits through brokers who actually go out and beat the bushes for accounts. The banks must pay them a fee in addition to the normal interest payable to the depositor. To meet these payments, banks have to make high-risk loans that pay higher interest. Often these loans are made outside the bank's usual business area and the bank simply doesn't know what it's doing. Only four closings, representing 7 percent of all failures, were due to inept management.

Beginning in 1971, the situation began to change noticeably. Larger and larger banks began to fail. And in the case of two of the three largest bank failures in American history, inept management was the cause.

The case of C. Arnholt Smith and the United States National Bank was a classic case of illegal and improper use of bank funds by ownership. And Smith had a lot of money to play with because deposits in his bank just about doubled between 1970 and its closing. These funds were not only from individuals but also from big savers who bought certificates of deposit. If a few of these certificates were not renewed, the bank could quickly run short of cash.

But Smith aggravated the situation by using the influx of funds to make loans to other enterprises of which he was the principal shareholder. That's called "self-dealing," and it's a bad banking practice. While directors' loans have usually been of the highest grade, when a principal owner begins making loans to himself, they are far more doubtful. When bank examiners visited the USNB in September 1971, "classified assets"—essentially potentially bad losses—amounted to 25 percent of the bank's capital and reserves. That's bad enough, but when the examiners came around again in June 1972, these assets amount to 371 percent of capital reserves. Almost nine-tenths of these assets were loans to Smith, his friends, his relatives, and their businesses.

Perhaps C. Arnholt Smith hoped that his good friend Richard M. Nixon could help him out if he ever ran into difficulty, but if he did, he was wrong. The Comptroller, who some believe should have acted far sooner on the basis of press reports about Smith's activities, finally moved in and forced Smith out of the bank. Besides suspicion that the Comptroller had acceded to Nixon administration pressures in delaying a declaration of insolvency, he was obviously responsible for the failure of his examiners to recognize that the firms to which the USNB was making loans just happened to be owned by Smith.

Of course, once the Comptroller began to worry about the USNB, his examiners were almost permanently on the scene trying to determine the exact state of health of the bank so that a decision could be made as to its ultimate disposition. The rest of the story has already been recounted.

In May 1974, the beginning of the collapse of New York's Franklin National Bank became public. In fact, the problem was not new or sudden. Like that of the USNB, the story of Franklin National showed the sad results of political involvement and the slow reaction time of the Comptroller.

Franklin National revealed in May 1974 that it would skip a dividend and that its profits had turned into losses because of setbacks in foreign-exchange transactions. Just as had the USNB, Franklin National had expanded rapidly. Originally a suburban Long Island bank, it had expanded first into New York City and then into international operations. In fact, it was ready for neither. As must all new banks, Franklin National accepted the riskier loans in order to corner a share of the New York market. Its entry into tricky foreign-exchange operations was prompted by Michele Sindona, who had purchased about one-fifth of Franklin National's shares.

Sindona, something of a mystery man of international banking, needed the approval of the Federal Reserve to hold both a large interest in Franklin National and a number of other business enterprises without their coming under permanent Fed supervision, which might have extended to requiring him to get rid of some of them as nonbank-related activities. Sindona wanted the Federal Reserve to determine that he did not hold a controlling interest in Franklin National.

Interestingly, Sindona's lawyer was a member of the firm of Mudge, Rose, Guthrie and Alexander, the former firm of

Richard Nixon and John Mitchell. In November 1972, just before the election, Sindona offered the Nixon reelection finance committee $1 million on the condition that the gift be kept anonymous. It was not accepted. To do so would have violated the provisions of the new campaign contribution law, which required full disclosure of sources after April 7, 1972.

By May 1973, Sindona and Franklin National were beginning to be regarded with some doubt by the Federal Reserve. It refused to allow the merger of the holding company that owned Franklin National and a finance company owned principally by Sindona. The Fed thought Franklin would be spreading itself too thin.

The Comptroller of the Currency might by now have been expected to be worrying about Franklin National. In July 1973, James E. Smith, a former lobbyist for the ABA, took over that office. He had served as a legislative liaison for Treasury Secretary David Kennedy, who, as it happens, was a friend and adviser of Sindona. Smith (no relation to C. Arnholt) felt he could not take action with respect to Franklin National as long as it was solvent. Even after the bank reported its big losses, passed its dividend, and saw trading in its stock suspended, Smith proclaimed that it was solvent.

After that news, however, Sindona did place his voting rights under Kennedy's control on the grounds that he was a person of "unquestionable integrity." Most people in the banking community thought that the move was mere window dressing, given Kennedy's long association with Sindona. Yet, throughout the summer, Smith sounded like a public-relations man for the bank, claiming that it was solvent and could stay in business.

Finally, as deposits continued to pour out of Franklin National, Smith was forced to admit that the bank was not solvent. He also admitted that he had been "remiss" in handling Franklin National because his office had not kept up with changes in the banking industry in the past decade. In October 1974, just one year after the USNB closing, the Comptroller and the FDIC closed Franklin National down and sold it. This time the European-American Bank picked up the pieces. The FDIC was left with a great many of the less desirable tidbits of the collapse of the twentieth largest bank in the United States. These were mostly loans that would be difficult, if not impossible, to collect.

It took only three months for the next giant to fall. Security National Bank, which also started out on Long Island, fell because it, too, had a large portfolio of bad loans resulting from too rapid expansion into New York City. When Security National began borrowing extensively from the Federal Reserve, Comptroller Smith wasted no time and began pushing the bank to find a merger partner. The Security directors were reluctant to let go, but Smith had already been badly burned by the Franklin National case.

Finally, Security went to Chemical Bank and asked what it would offer. Chemical, which had already put a team together at the time of bidding on Franklin National, was ready to make a rapid judgment on Security. Within ten days it said it was ready to gobble up the forty-fourth largest bank in the United States.

Next?

All of this gave a lot of people the willies. In fact, it had become so much a matter of concern that a Boston rock group named itself "Why Banks Fail" and was an immediate hit. People were obviously worried that banks would fail as they had during the Depression. Could they lose the savings they thought were the safest?

The short answer is no. Deposit insurance really does work. Under the FDIC, each depositor is now insured for up to $40,000 to cover each account bearing his or her name. A *New Yorker* cartoon, published at the time of great worry, showed a bank with a sign in its window, reading: "Only money in the bank is like money in the bank."

Almost no bank, except a very small one, is likely to be a total shambles. When there is something of value to salvage and where state laws permit, the failing bank will almost certainly be acquired by a stronger bank. Depositors will hardly know the difference. If that doesn't happen, the FDIC will dip into its funds to come up with enough money to protect insured deposits. Admittedly, the FDIC has less than $6 billion, and with such big failures, people might worry about there being enough to make good on the insurance.

It would take a mighty big bust to run out the string on the FDIC. But should that happen, the Federal Reserve could do now what it could not do during the Great Depression—print more money. As people came into the bank to close their accounts, checking and savings money could be turned into cash money. This might actually result in less money rather than more. And once people got the psychological satisfaction of "touching" their money, they would probably stop closing their accounts. In short, both the Fed and the FDIC have learned that in case of serious problems, their action does not save banks so much as it saves the whole economy.

So while the average person can be assured about the consequences of bank failure, he or she has every right to wonder why bigger banks are failing more frequently and why the closings are due increasingly to bad management.

It's possible that bank management is no worse now than it has ever been since the Depression. But never, since then, has the economy been in such trouble. As we'll see later, the money supply was consciously reduced as a way of fighting inflation, and then a major recession took over. A slowdown in the economy inevitably weeds out the financially weak, and some of them undoubtedly owe banks money. When they can't pay, the banks find themselves short of needed cash. Banks that are sufficiently diversified and have avoided too many high-risk loans can ride out hard times. The banks where bad management judgments have been made are under greater pressure.

Many banks, but especially those which run into trouble, have taken part in a recent trend in financing loans that amount to a significant change in banking practices. In the past, loans were not allowed to outstrip deposits. But with loan demands increasing in recent years and the banks' desire to maximize profits, they have gone out into the market themselves to borrow money to relend. As opposed to deposit money, this is "hot money." The bank knows that it will have to make good on its loan—money on which it may be paying more interest than on deposits. If the bank's own loans run into trouble, it still must pay back the money it has borrowed. A bank may be tempted to go too far into loans backed by "hot money," and the Comptroller doesn't like to see the amount involved go beyond 6 percent of assets. But this can be a dangerous business.

Indeed, despite all the regulation of banks, they can take a great many risks affecting their depositors' money. The regulators cannot stop banks from currency speculation. They cannot prevent unwise loans, although they may end up pumping funds into the banks to make sure that the banks themselves are not closed down because of the weakness of their customers. Since 1970, when the Federal Reserve poured money into the banking system to ensure that Penn Central would not be allowed to bring down the entire economy because it couldn't pay back its loans, the Federal Reserve has been in the business of covering doubtful loans, not to save the companies concerned or even the bank, but the economy as a whole. But this is clearly a case of the supposed regulator being "used" by a situation instead of keeping it under control.

Thus, there are some major loopholes in what regulators regulate, because banks are doing things they haven't done before. Above all, they themselves are behaving more like businesses and less like public utilities.

Reforming the Comptroller

The other obvious problem is with how the regulators do their job. The members of the Federal Reserve Board, the chairman of the FDIC, and the Comptroller of the Currency are all politically appointed, but only the Comptroller turns out to be a political figure most of the time. Perhaps that's because the Federal Reserve Board is just that—a board—and professionals—economists, bankers, and businessmen—have been appointed to it. The chairman of the FDIC is also a member of a board on which the Comptroller sits, and again the tradition has been to name a professional. The Comptroller exercises his functions without benefit of any checks and thus may try to make a name for himself by flashy decision-making. In cases of bad judgment, there's nobody who can overrule him, even the Treasury Secretary to whom he nominally reports.

While it might make sense to take a look at the complex Federal regulatory system that now exists with a view to some streamlining of functions, there's a great deal to be said for allowing specialized agencies to carry out specialized functions. If a single, unified agency were incompetent, there would be no other lines of defense.

For the time being, it would seem wise to break with precedent and create a Board of Administrators of the National Banks to replace the Comptroller of the Currency (except maybe for the limited function of controlling the currency, which is mostly a historic relic). The board should be financed, at least in part, by Congress. Now the Comptroller is totally independent of Congress because his operation is financed by a levy of banks. He is not, therefore, totally independent of them. With staggered terms that would help insulate the board from political pressures, and with different backgrounds, the members might be able to avoid the excesses of a James Saxon, who wanted to change national banking on a whim, or a James Smith, who had a soft spot for weak banks.

An Economics Lesson: The Federal Reserve

While all of the regulatory agencies affect people at least indirectly, one of them has a powerful and far more direct impact on their lives. This is the Federal Reserve, known in financial circles as the Fed, which has the task of controlling the supply of money in the American economy. Sometimes banks are blamed, as in the case of high interest rates, when a development is really the result of a conscious policy of the Fed.

We all recognize that there's more to money than simply coin and currency. Banks can actually create money by putting on their books a credit to the account of somebody who, for example, has just been granted a loan. That person is not actually given cash but may make withdrawals from a loan account by writing checks that are accepted as though they were cash. Just how much money a bank can create in this way is determined by the amount of reserves it holds.

Reserves take one of three forms. First, reserve dollars may be created by gold or "paper gold." "Paper gold," or special drawing rights, is now accepted to settle debts among countries just as gold itself is. Each country has a certain amount of paper gold in relation to the amount of gold and dollars it holds. Paper gold has become more accepted around the world as the dollar, whittled down in value by inflation, has become less desirable. When gold or paper gold flows into the United States, the selling country gets dollars, which are credited to its account at the Federal Reserve Bank of New York. When those dollars are spent in the United States they move into other banks where they can be counted as part of the reserves that the Fed requires them to hold.

A second source of reserves is, of course, money in circulation. Actually, because of population growth, more cash has been needed in circulation, leaving less that the banks could hold as reserves. Neither these reserves nor dollars resulting from gold transactions can be controlled by national policy. Naturally, more money could be printed, but that would represent, in any case, only a small part of the total reserves necessary to back the enormous money supply of almost $1 trillion. Because these two sources of reserve money can fluctuate on their own, the Federal Reserve was given other more sophisticated instruments that enable it to influence directly the amount of reserves.

Most required cash reserves are held by banks in their reserve accounts with the Federal Reserve banks. If the Fed makes a loan to a member bank, it will increase the reserve account by the amount of the loan. That increases a bank's reserves. The interest charged by the Fed is called the discount rate.

In addition to making or refusing to make loans to banks, the Fed can also influence the overall amount of reserves by its investment policy, known as open-market operations. If a Federal Reserve bank purchases a government security, it pays by check to the seller, who deposits that check in his bank. When the check comes back to the Fed, that amount is credited to the bank's reserve account, thus reducing its reserves. The decision to buy or sell government securities is made on the basis of the Fed's decision whether it wishes to increase bank reserves or not.

Where does the Fed get the money to lend and invest? Like any other lender or investor, the Fed hopes to make a profit on its loans in the form of interest, and on its investments in the form of a higher selling price than purchase price. Its excess profits go to the United States Treasury.

The Fed has two additional tools for influencing reserves. It can set the interest rate it charges on loans—the discount rate. By raising the rate, it can discourage banks from borrowing to grant loans and thus prevent their reserves from growing. In the past twenty years, the discount rate has fluctuated considerably, with an overall low of 1.5 percent and a high of 8 percent. Each time the discount rate sinks back, it never goes back quite as far as where it started from.

The reserve requirements—the amount of reserves banks must have as a percentage of their checking and savings accounts—can also be varied by the Fed. When the dollar-reserve requirement is lowered, that means that one reserve dollar will back more dollars created by the bank. If the reserve requirement is increased, each reserve dollar backs fewer dollars available for loans. The Fed does not, in practice, vary this rate too widely, with large banks having being required during the last twenty years to hold between 16.5 percent and 18 percent of the checkbook deposits in reserve.

It's obvious that by determining the amount of reserves banks have—most frequently through its open-market operations—the Fed actually determines to a considerable extent just how much money there is. It can safely be presumed that banks will create as much money as the Fed allows.

During periods of "easy money," the Fed may be lending more to banks, investing more in government securities, and lowering the reserve requirements and the discount rate (indeed, it could not lend more without lowering the interest rate on those loans). Because banks pay lower prices for their reserves, they can charge their customers lower prices for the money they lend. The Fed may adopt such an easy-money policy when it wants to restart a sluggish economy where unemployment is high and business activity is in a slump.

The only problem with an easy-money policy is that it's hard to know when money has become too easy. Then there is more money around than there are goods to be bought. When money chases goods, inflation results; that is, the price of goods becomes artificially high because of their relative shortage.

At this point the Fed will embark on a "tight-money" policy. It will sell government securities, the reserve requirement may be increased, the discount rate will be raised, and thus the amount of loans to banks will be cut. As a result, the amount of reserves will decline and each reserve dollar will back fewer dollars at the banks. Because banks have to pay high interest for their reserves, they will charge high interest for their loans as a way of discouraging would-be borrowers.

Frequently, in recent years, people have blamed the banks for high interest rates. Here was one kind of inflation that could be remedied if only the banks would be willing to make smaller profits and lower their interest rates. What those people do not realize is that the high interest rates are the result of a Fed policy. Of course, that policy has the effect of contributing to inflation itself.

Banks have been ingenious in devising ways to get around Fed rules and policies in order to keep on lending to the many borrowers who will pay any price for a loan. For many, their foreign operations have been a source of funds that escape Federal controls.

Finally, the entire economy begins to slow down because of the inability of people to pay the high prices that are charged. When they stop buying cars, cars stop getting more expensive, but at the same time, auto workers may lose their jobs. Thus, a tight-money policy can lead back to the need for an easy-money policy—to get the economy moving again.

Of course, the Fed's monetary policy is not the only way the government can influence the economy. The levels of government spending and of taxation also have a powerful impact. However, during the Nixon years, the administration largely abandoned these measures of "fiscal" policy and left the Fed to try to keep the economy on an even keel through its monetary policy.

Obviously, the big problem for the Fed is knowing when to shift gears. If it keeps an easy-money policy too long, it can bring on inflation. If it keeps a tight-money policy too long, it can bring on recession. It has to be looking ahead and trying not only to solve the crisis of the moment but also to be seeking the proper method of returning to an even keel. It should also be attempting to close loopholes that allow banks to evade their obligations to fall in line with Fed policy. But the Fed has not been aggressive in doing this.

The Fed has taken a lot of criticism recently for its failure to change gears at the right time. In part, this is a bum rap, because most economists would argue that the Fed should not be left by itself to try to influence the economy, that there should be a "mix" of fiscal and monetary policy. In recent years, government policy has been like a car with one front wheel that can be turned; the other just keeps going straight ahead. That causes a lot of drag and makes it difficult to control the car—or the economy.

The authority for the Fed to control monetary policy comes from the Congress, which has been reluctant to try to take a collective guess on monetary policy. But as discontent with the Fed's handling of monetary policy rises, the

Congress obviously becomes more tempted to intervene or at least give the Fed some direct orders.

From the individual's viewpoint, the bank is actually an instrument of a major national policy to influence the economy. So the whopping loan rate on a new car may be more than a symptom of bad times; it may be part of the cure.

9 There's a Great Day Coming

American banking has evolved just about as much as the American automobile. The car was first powered by the internal combustion engine, and it still is. The basic design of the car has actually changed little, and it hasn't become much safer over the years.

By the same token, the business of banking hasn't developed much since 1933. The only big change is that, like cars, bank facilities are now accessible to a greater number of people. And in the same way that a degree of auto safety has been forced on manufacturers, the banks have been required to provide their customers with more information and to reduce outright discrimination.

The real revolution in banking lies ahead. It will come gradually, in line with the ability of the mammoth financial sector to absorb change. Banks will increasingly take advantage of technology to streamline their procedures and eliminate the billions of pieces of paper that threaten to dominate and ultimately choke the financial system. Government will alter the conditions of competition, removing artificial requirements that are relics of a historical evolution, and thus increasing the choices available to the consumer. In addition, passage of the Truth-in-Lending and Fair Credit Billing Acts and the creation of consumer offices in banking regulatory agencies indicate that government is becoming increasingly aware of inequities in the treatment of customers. But the consumer, too, must be better educated, both to take advantage of the services that exist and to protect himself when disclosure is inadequate or practices are illegal.

You and the Computer

From the consumer's viewpoint, the biggest changes in banking result from the advent of the computer. Just as the check has replaced cash as the principal medium of exchange, the computer entry will replace the check for many transactions. With the card providing access to the computer system, banking will pass from the age of paper to the age of plastic.

The bank card is the opening wedge. Its more traditional function is to provide credit. A purchase can be made without the instant outlay of cash. Indeed, a purchase need not be covered by funds then in the bank account.

Even more significant over the long run is the access the card gives to cash. It means the end of bankers' hours. The card is already being used in conjunction with banking machines that can take the place of the teller for a great many operations. At present, the automatic teller is used mostly to provide cash at any time of day or night. Yet it has disadvantages. It performs no other functions, it is not conveniently located, it provides only a limited amount of cash each day, and it involves an additional charge.

All of these inconveniences may disappear. Clearly, automatic tellers will be able to carry out a variety of services—perhaps as many as 90 percent of all transactions now carried out by tellers. Transfers among accounts, loan repayment, and even bill paying are possible through the use of the properly equipped automatic teller. If these machines become more accessible and more heavily used, banking, one of the most labor-intensive industries, will at last begin to realize the economies of automation. Some of those savings should be passed on to the consumer.

The most important next step will be something called DPD—Direct Pay Deposit. Instead of paying each employee individually, employers deposit pay directly into the employee's account. The employee receives the paycheck stub, with the complete information on deductions, either directly from the bank or from the employer in the traditional way. The employee is no longer put to any inconvenience in obtaining his paycheck and is not required to take it to the bank in order to obtain cash. There are no lost or stolen checks, and the money is credited even if the employee is away from work. From the bank's viewpoint, the employee is a more attractive credit customer because of the continuous and permanent relationship created by DPD. And for Social Security and welfare recipients, the system eliminates waiting for the regular check in the mail.

This system is already in use in many places. While it provides added convenience to the depositor, its greatest significance is that it opens the door to a great variety of other services. While DPD has traditionally been limited to deposits that are simple transfers from the employer's bank account to the employee's account in the same bank, now it is possible for the money to be credited to an account in another bank. New Automated Clearing Houses, which allow for transfers among participating banks through a common computer arrangement, are budding all over the country. Once this arrangement exists for the purpose of crediting paychecks, all of the customers of all the participating banks can be linked to each other through the computer.

The next step is the preauthorized transfer. This, too, is not really a new idea because checking account customers have long been able to direct the bank to make automatic deposits in a savings account. The concept can be expanded to authorize the bank, once it has received your pay deposit, to pay automatically certain fixed and regular bills such as your mortgage, insurance premiums, or consumer loan payments. The bother of writing checks and the risk of late penalty charges would be eliminated. It would even save on postage. Such a system would also be possible for payments of regular bills even if the amount varied from month to month. Of course, if customers encountered billing inaccuracies from the power company, for example, they would not want to have their electric bills paid in this way. Yet the kinds of bills that could be paid is almost limitless, ranging from the oil company's budget plan to property taxes.

Two other innovations will make it possible for consumers to use electronic funds transfer instead of the traditional check. The multicheck is already in use in some places. A depositor instructs the bank to make payments to a number of merchants by means of a single document. With the Automated Clearing House system, a great many merchants can be covered. Both cost and effort would be reduced for the customer.

The bill-check works in about the same way, but only involves a single merchant. He sends the customer a bill, part of which is actually a check. The customer fills out the check to indicate how much he wishes to pay. When he is ready to pay the bill, he returns the bill-check to the merchant, who can then enter it into the banking system. The flexibility provided the customer is especially appropriate for one-time and variable charges, where the consumer wishes to review the bill and withhold payment until he has enough money in his checking account to cover it and his other expected needs. The bill-check saves the customer the trouble of writing a check.

Once electronic funds transfer is available, a variety of uses becomes evident. In Lincoln, Nebraska, customers of Hinky Dinky supermarkets can withdraw money from their savings accounts with the First Federal Savings and Loan Association when they are ready to pay at the checkout counter. This enables them to earn interest on "checking account money" right up to the moment they need to use it. The store simply has a computer terminal that can almost instantly verify the customer's account information and balance and transfer the funds. The Hinky Dinky personnel give the customer a bank record of the transaction. Similar systems were set up by 14 commercial banks in 9 states and 117 savings and loans in 17 states within months of the Hinky Dinky plan's inauguration.

At the Farmers and Mechanics Savings Bank in Minneapolis, perhaps the most sophisticated use of plastic credit is being tested. Called Pay by Phone, it turns the customer's home or office telephone into a computer terminal. Using a push-button telephone, the customer transmits instructions directly to the bank's computer about payments he wishes to have made to participating merchants. A number of codes are used to ensure security. The customer receives a daily statement showing transactions, and each merchant receives a consolidated payment from the bank. This system enables the depositor to collect interest on funds until they are needed. The thrift gains deposits that would otherwise have remained in noninterest-bearing commercial accounts. More popular are the various bank-by-phone plans, where the customer gives instructions orally to a phone teller. What is more significant about this process is the radical reduction in the amount of paperwork. The bank is given an order by the customer, withdraws funds from one account and deposits them to another, and prints confirming statements, all automatically.

Perhaps the ultimate step is the point-of-sale service. Already tested by the City National Bank of Columbus, Ohio, this system will permit a customer to present a card at the store at the time of purchase. The card is not the traditional credit card. It is a "debit" or "cash" card, because it enables the purchaser to debit his own account and transfer payment to the store automatically. Use of the card would also make more traditional transactions easy. If you chose to pay by check, the card would be inserted into a terminal connected to your bank's computer that would verify that you had sufficient money in your account to cover the bill without the cumbersome procedure of presenting several pieces of identification to the salesperson. In the case of merchandise to be shipped, you might prefer to make a credit purchase and the card would then serve the function of a normal retail credit card.

The consumer should find that point-of-sale bank service could do everything from eliminating bounced checks (checks would be eliminated and the funds would be transferred immediately) to earning a cash discount, now reported to be at 2 percent, for actually ordering the transfer. What's more, waiting time in line should be cut, because there would be no checking of identification, no completion of forms. The process could take a matter of seconds. And bankers' hours would be of absolutely no relevance; the bank would always be open.

In addition to convenience, electronic funds transfer would push us a lot closer to the cashless society. If nothing else, that should reduce muggings, because no cash would be used at any point. Even bank robbers would be likely to find far less cash in the vault.

The greatest disadvantage is that the customer is forced to deal with a machine, not people. Many people place a high premium on dealing with a small, local bank because they come to know the personnel and expect personal service. If there are any problems concerning an account, the customer can expect them to be resolved by people he knows. While people are quick to recognize the benefits of the dial telephone, those who remember when the operator asked: "Number, please?" recall that they were not at all unhappy with a system that provided them a degree of human contact.

In addition, the general public attitude toward computers is far from favorable. Stories of checks being sent out in the wrong amount or of people being harassed for nonpayment of an astronomical bill they did not incur leave a feeling of mistrust and real concern about being left at the mercy of the computer. In addition, the Equity Funding scandal demonstrated that the public may, in future years, have more to worry about because of sophisticated electronics defrauders than because of muggers. In that case, company officials were able to use the computer to record thousands of insurance policies, which, in fact, had never been sold. This false information artificially inflated the company's assets, enabling it to make unjustified loans. The real losers in such a case could be the honest customers—in the case of a bank, its depositors. While the regulators would have to be able to cope with such a fraud, it is clear that today they do not have the capacity to do so and that there may be no known method of defeating certain kinds of fraud.

Consumers also believe that where a new and simpler

system is installed, there should be economic benefits. They believe that banks profit from electronic innovations and that some of that gain should be returned in the form of lower charges.

Electronic funds transfer can, by its very nature, end up costing the customer money. Because funds can be transferred instantly, the "float" will be eliminated. For the individual, "float" means that you can write a check on Saturday without having the funds to cover it in your account. Then, the following Monday, you can deposit enough to cover the check when it is presented for collection. Of course, both banks and merchants will also lose the advantages of the "float." Customers for whom electronics are supposed to improve service will not be happy about losing the "float."

Customer resistance is now the greatest obstacle to an electronic funds transfer system. A national commission has been created by Congress to deal with this new phenomenon, but its membership has more representatives of the banking industry than of consumers. Only when banks can prove that the new system is virtually error-free and protects individual privacy, and that lower charges compensate for the lack of personal contact and the loss of the "float," will consumers be ready to accept the coming revolution in banking.

A New Structure for Banking

With the exception of the oil industry, perhaps no other industry has been the subject of so much scrutiny, official and academic, as banking. Although the findings of all of these studies do not agree in every detail, they all indicate the need to revise the banking structure as it has evolved over the years. Artificial distinctions between institutions and services stifle competition and thus limit the choices available to consumers.

Three major studies have been conducted by the Federal government. The Presidential Commission on Financial Structure and Regulation, more frequently known as the Hunt Commission because it was headed by Reed O. Hunt, former chairman of Crown Zellerbach, was published in December 1971. The approach of this study is admittedly that of the banking institutions themselves, not of consumers. In fact, one member, Lane Kirkland of the AFL-CIO, refused even to sign the report because of its slant. Yet the Hunt Commission report was surprising in that bankers were willing to admit the need for major structural changes.

In August 1973, Congress provided its response. In a staff report prepared for the House Committee on Banking and Currency, headed by Wright Patman, long a critic of banks, a far more consumer-oriented series of proposals was made.

Finally, late that month, the White House and the Treasury published their own suggestions, which took the form of draft legislation. Perhaps this was the most surprising of the three documents, because the White House was prepared to back significant changes in the banking structure.

These proposals on the Federal level spurred considerable state activity, and financial reform became the topic of the hour. In New York, the Banking Department created its own version of the Hunt Commission, while the New York Federal Reserve Bank came up with a study and recommendations specifically related to mutual savings banks.

Reform has focused on limits on interest payments and restrictions on the functions of thrift institutions. Probably it was the thrifts themselves that prompted this concern, because of the creation of NOW accounts—in effect, checking accounts on which interest is paid. Because of the novelty of what turned out to be a perfectly legal act, Congress quickly limited NOW accounts to Massachusetts and New Hampshire, the two states where they were first established. But in order to freeze the accounts, Congress was forced to argue that they were an experiment and the results would have to be analyzed before they would be opened elsewhere. At best, that amounted to a holding action while the various study commissions could come up with suggestions on how to deal with the new conditions of competition.

The interest-paying checking account, by whatever name it may be called, appears inevitable. Even the Treasury legislation provides for it in the form of the NOW account, on which the bank may technically require that the depositor wait 30 days before having his money. This is a mere technicality, and there is no practical difference between the NOW account and the traditional demand-deposit account, on which interest would still be banned.

Clearly, the payment of interest on checking accounts would move the relationship between the bank and consumer closer to the notion of fee-for-service. The customer would be compensated for leaving his funds in a checking account. But the almost certain corollary of this development would be the ultimate lifting of interest-rate ceilings on both commercial banks and thrifts.

The differential in rates between banks and thrifts was designed to ensure that savings institutions would have enough funds to finance mortgages. Commercial banks have long smarted under this distinction and argue that they assume a portion of the mortgage loan even now. They favor open competition on equal terms for the saver's dollar. If the interest rates paid went up, so would the cost of mortgages. If resistance to high mortgage rates by home buyers began to be felt, the interest rate on savings would have to be adjusted. In short, the market rather than government regulators would establish interest rates. Of course, through its continued impact on monetary policy, the Federal Reserve could also influence, though not control, interest rates.

Because each step of reform leads to another, thrift institutions are gradually being allowed to take on more of the functions of commercial banks. Of course, they may also have to give up many of the advantages they enjoy as compared with commercial banks and maintain reserves on the same basis. Equity would require that if thrifts lost their advantage in paying higher interest than banks, they should gain the advantages of being able to provide the same kinds of services.

Savings and loans and mutual savings banks would acquire the authority to provide checking accounts. In addition, they would probably be able to offer personal loans in relatively small amounts, an activity that has generally been prohibited to them. The thrifts might also be permitted to provide a number of other services such as selling mutual funds, financial counseling, management of trusts and estates, and supervision of real-estate investment trusts. Indeed, it would be possible for these thrifts to convert to stock ownership and even to become commercial banks, as they came to provide the same services.

This step-by-step development, from paying interest on checking accounts to eliminating the distinction between banks and thrifts, may seem inevitable and logical. How well it serves the consumer interest remains to be seen. In particular, the distinction among institutions may have served to increase rather than limit choice. Because mutual savings banks see the world differently from commercial banks, they may provide the kinds of services that some customers feel they cannot obtain at the bank where they maintain a checking account. The competitive urge to develop services not provided elsewhere could diminish in a situation where all institutions were alike.

Whatever the ultimate evolution of commercial banks and the thrifts, the recent studies have focused new attention on the unique role played by credit unions. As a result, proposals have been aimed at strengthening them without necessarily turning them into commercial banks. Credit unions are closely circumscribed because of their exemption from Federal taxes. As lending organizations among "friends," they are designed to reduce illegal loan-shark operations. In addition, they have no stockholders who must be paid a share of the profits, and thus there are no profits. Whatever is earned in interest is returned to savers and borrowers. Provided these conditions are maintained, even though services are increased, credit unions should be able to avoid increased taxation.

Above all, credit unions will continue to be open only to members of affinity groups such as members of the same church or employees of the same firm. While some states allow mere geographical residence in the same state to qualify a group to form a credit union, recent proposals call for closer ties in the future. On the other hand, starting a credit union is not very difficult, and the Credit Union National Association provides advice. The amount of funds required for the operation of a credit union is not large. Thus, those who might be eligible for membership in a newly created credit union should be encouraged to investigate the undertaking.

Credit unions are now authorized to offer checking accounts, just as other financial institutions do. In addition, they will also be able to service larger loans than are now permitted. Just how high this ceiling might be raised depends on the length of time for which the credit unions would be prepared to make loans. In general, they have made loans for relatively short periods, but when loan amounts increase, so do loan durations. In 1977, credit unions were authorized to write mortgage loans. And if interest-rate ceilings are lifted for banks and thrifts, they will probably also be lifted for credit unions.

The new banking structure is perhaps more likely to have a positive effect on the consumer than the introduction of electronic funds transfers. Over the past few years, both have been gradually phased in, although there is still a long way to go. In addition to consumer resistance to the computer, banks have found that electronic methods are expensive. At the same time, they have learned more about coping with the veritable torrent of checks that are produced every day. It appears that the number of checks in use is increasing less rapidly. As a result, while the computer has transformed banking, introduction of more electronic aids is likely to be slowed.

But the process of eliminating the distinctions between various kinds of financial institutions continues. Of course, those banks that have enjoyed certain competitive advantages are unhappy with the changes. The object of this process is to stimulate competition in the kinds of services available and their costs. Once again, the consumer should be the chief beneficiary of increased competition.

Branching Out: Delivering Bank Services

Over the years, the barriers against statewide branching have been falling. The tide toward large banks with many branches or subsidiaries seems irreversible. The day of the unit bank is fading, and with it the familiarity that came of everybody in town knowing the bank president and the entire staff. If there is any advantage to this trend, it is that banking services are being offered in more convenient locations. But it would seem unwise for bank regulators to simply abandon any limits on branching. Expansion into unprofitable branches could endanger all customers because inevitably the bank would be weakened financially.

Some bank regulators and officials believe that state lines are artificial barriers to bank competition. Under existing law, it is now impossible for a bank to extend its operations across state lines except for representative offices that can be used to solicit business for the home bank. Now New York, the nation's financial capital, is considering approaching other states to allow interstate banking on terms of reciprocity. The use of interstate branches or subsidiaries would be attractive to New York banks, which are eager to gain access to the large and growing market in states such as California. Obviously, the major New York banks are confident they could withstand competition in their home market from out-of-state banks. But even some smaller states would favor interstate banking as a way of attracting a portion of the large pools of capital held by major banks elsewhere into their own economic plans.

At the same time, branch banking will take on a new meaning with the use of automatic tellers. Regulators will probably not consider them ordinary branches. Already the Comptroller has said that banks in one state can place automatic tellers in another, although this ruling has been challenged. This is the first step in recent years toward interstate banking. And a bank will have to make less of a capital expenditure to reach an even greater number of people than if it had been required to create an entirely new branch.

Mortgages and Trusts

Both mortgage and trust services are likely to come in for more critical review.

The crisis in mortgage money availability resulting from high interest rates and the portion of loan portfolios composed of older, lower-interest mortgages has fueled a debate over variable-rate mortgages. The interest rate would change over time to reflect changing interest rates in the marketplace. Banks and thrifts argue that variable-rate mortgages are fair to the borrower and ensure a steady supply of funds for the mortgage market at all times.

Consumers see variable-rate mortgages quite differently. The mortgage loan is almost certainly the largest borrowing by an individual in a lifetime. Repayment of that loan becomes a permanent part of family budgeting over the long haul. To have the amount that is to be repaid constantly shifting could have a major disruptive effect on the budget. In addition, the Patman report attacks the proposal on the ground that it shifts all of the risk from the lender to the borrower and that it will probably discourage homeownership. Patman reports that if payments were kept level, the term of the mortgage would have to be varied and that as little as a 1-percent rate increase could transform a 30-year mortgage into one running forever. The Hunt Commission, which favors variable rates as an option for VA and FHA mortgages, admits that the borrower has few alternatives in obtaining a mortgage and would be unlikely to bargain with the bank. Thus, even the Hunt Commission suggests that the terms of such mortgages be carefully explained in advance and that borrowers be given the option of terminating the variable-rate system at any time they become unhappy with it.

In 1975, the Federal Home Loan Bank Board proposed

authorizing variable-rate mortgages that could not increase more than 2.5 percent over the life of the mortgage loan or 0.5 percent in any six months. Under pressure from consumer and minority groups and from organized labor, Congress moved to block this proposal from being implemented.

Home Savings and Loan in Los Angeles, the largest savings and loan, is already making variable-rate loans. And balloon mortgages, such as offered by New York's East River Savings Bank, amount to much the same thing. Banks and thrifts say they may have to go this route, whatever consumers want, just to be able to make mortgage loans. Of course, such statements indicating that the only kind of mortgage loans they will be able to offer will be unpopular with consumers, may be nothing more than a form of pressure intended to convince the government to subsidize mortgage loans by paying part of the interest.

Both state usury laws and ceilings on government-backed mortgages dry up mortgage money. When interest rates rise to or above these levels, banks and thrifts simply refuse to make loans below these ceilings when they can make other loans at higher rates. Numerous proposals have been made to allow these rates to move in relation to the general level of interest rates instead of having them set by law. While these proposals seem reasonable, some may wonder if the existence of such limits does not serve to brake somewhat a flight toward even higher interest rates.

The abuses of trust departments have brought the Hunt Commission to the point of making recommendations that would substantially transform their operations. The commission favors a wall between trust and commercial departments when total trust assets exceed $200 million. In addition to calling for closer regulation, the commission would require an annual report detailing stockholdings, dollar values, and interlocking directorates. The Patman report goes even further and proposes "the complete separation of trust departments from commercial banks, except possibly for the very smallest trust departments." Clearly, concern about trust department inefficiency and disregard for the interests of the beneficiaries is increasing and has reached the banking industry itself, as shown by the Hunt Commission report.

Reforming the Regulators

Regulation itself comes in for reform under the various proposals. Patman suggested that finance companies engaged in interstate business be subject to Federal chartering. He and others foresaw similar treatment for mutual savings banks and savings and loans owned by stockholders.

At the same time, some proposals call for a single Federal regulator and others for a rationalization of the current system in which three Federal agencies—the Comptroller of the Currency, the Federal Reserve, and the Federal Deposit Insurance Corporation—share regulatory responsibility over commercial banks, and other agencies deal with savings and loans and credit unions.

Consumers will be less concerned about the form of regulatory supervision than its results. Clearly, the present system in which the Comptroller, a politically oriented official, has the ultimate authority over the largest commercial banks has proved to be inadequate if not downright dangerous to the public interest. But consumers would do well to be suspicious of the panacea of a single Federal regulator. If that regulator did as poorly as the Comptroller, without being subject to pressure from other agencies, the consumer might well be even more poorly served. While the studies have not dealt with state regulation, a good case can be made for strengthening such regulation on the obvious grounds that it is closer to the people who interests must be protected.

Finally, the debate over the Federal Reserve's independence in determining monetary policy can be expected to continue unabated. Patman maintained that the Federal Reserve should be required to set monetary policy in the light of guidelines laid down by the President. In addition, Congress could strengthen its own authority over the

Federal Reserve by the power of the purse if it were made dependent on appropriations rather than contributions from member banks. Although Patman is no longer the central figure on the House Banking Committee, his views have gained increasing acceptance as the tight-money policies used by the Fed to combat inflation have been blamed for the ensuing recession. While the Fed's policies are certainly worthy of criticism, there is no indication of superior wisdom either in the White House or on Capitol Hill. In effect, the Fed has been attacked for failing to do what others did not do.

The Consumer and the Bank

In a recent study for the American Bankers Association, a survey organization found increased consumer skepticism about banks. "While the image of banks as solid and reliable still exists," it said, "it is in the process of change. In-depth interview results indicate that many respondents have gradually come to view banks as large, impersonal, bureaucratic, even exploitive institutions."

Of course, banks have been changing in recent years. Surprisingly, only in the past decade have they come to regard themselves as businesses. The growth of assets has become their dominant goal. As a result, in many cases, customers have felt that services were actually reduced or that charges were increased. In general, smaller banks have not gone along with this trend as rapidly as major institutions.

At the same time, bank customers have become more consumer oriented. Where previously they felt it improper to question bank policies and even doubted that there were differences among banks, they now are more concerned with looking out for themselves. Bank policies are watched with more suspicion and doubt, and the collapse of Franklin National raised real fears about the ability of bank managers.

The survey done by the ABA reveals a broad spectrum

of discontent. Customers believe that management is rigid and that dealing with a bank is like dealing with the government bureaucracy. They complain about inadequate staffing and about the rapid turnover of the poorly paid bank personnel most of us come in contact with regularly. Even bankers' hours, certainly nothing new, draw a lot of negative comment. Customers feel that the bank's hours suit the management and the employees far more than the consumer. People who have been used to dealing with local bank officers are unhappy with branch banking, because the local manager may have to check with the main office on decisions that previously could easily have been made at the local office.

Perhaps most important, customers complain that they cannot obtain information about bank services and help in dealing with everything from balancing checking accounts to reading statements and passbooks. The cold, businesslike attitude of the bank coupled with the frequent refusal to disclose information that would help the customer make an informed decision has led to the kind of reaction of one person interviewed: "We don't trust our institutions today. . . . The institutions are getting bigger and man is getting smaller."

Help is on the way. With cumbersome slowness, public institutions are gradually beginning to recognize consumer demand for better service from financial institutions. Even those who would question the need for a growing government bureaucracy can see that a regulatory system that is largely self-enforcing—where the consumer himself can take action if the bank or thrift fails to follow the law—is both economical and desirable.

The first step, and probably the most important, is disclosure. That does not mean more fine print. Instead, it means more explanation and more attention to informing the customer of the meaning of those explanations. For the moment, banks seem to have adopted the attitude that it's better to take the money and run than to take a chance on a friendlier attitude toward their customers. There is no proof that banks would do worse using a more open approach. If they continue to spurn it, the government will inevitably be pushed to lay down stringent disclosure requirements.

But the consumer's best safeguard remains himself. Only Oregon makes consumer education a part of the public-school curriculum. Without such schooling, it's up to the consumer to get whatever information he can about the places where his money goes.

This book contains at least seventy-five specific suggestions that should help consumers make the most of their money. To a great extent, it provides the kind of disclosure that should already be available from banks. Just how much money these suggestions are worth depends on the financial activities of each individual—his or her checking account, credit card, personal loan, mortgage, trust account. But there is almost no adult who does not have some relationship with a bank, and virtually all can save money by knowing more about how banks operate. Even if you forget every one of the specific points in this book, you should not hesitate to ask questions at the bank. If you don't understand a service, or it seems unfair, ask and keep on asking questions until you get a solid answer. But before you even set foot in the bank, decide for yourself exactly what service you need. You may be surprised to find that it exists.

As Thoreau said, most men lead lives of quiet desperation. Today the struggle against impersonal institutions only increases that feeling. But there is no reason to be intimidated by banks. You are the customer, and you have the right to know. If you don't learn the right questions and then ask them, what you don't know can hurt you.

Appendix 1

Who to Contact for Help in Dealing with a Bank

Your State Bank Regulator

ALABAMA
Superintendent of Banks
651 Administration Building
64 North Union Street
Montgomery, Alabama 36104

ALASKA
Director of Banking and Securities
Department of Commerce
Pouch D
Juneau, Alaska 99801

ARIZONA
Superintendent of Banks
101 Commerce Building
1601 West Jefferson Street
Phoenix, Arizona 85007

ARKANSAS
Bank Commissioner
Suite 700
University Tower Building
12th and University
Little Rock, Arkansas 72204

CALIFORNIA
Superintendent of Banks
Suite 750
235 Montgomery Street
San Francisco, California 94104

COLORADO
State Bank Commissioner
325 State Office Building
Denver, Colorado 80203

CONNECTICUT
Bank Commissioner
State Office Building
Hartford, Connecticut 06115

DELAWARE
State Banking Commissioner
Post Office Box 657
Dover, Delaware 19901

FLORIDA
State Comptroller
Capitol Building
Tallahassee, Florida 32304

GEORGIA
Commissioner of Banking and Finance
122 State Capitol Building
Atlanta, Georgia 30334

GUAM
Banking Commissioner
Government of Guam
Agana, Guam 96910

HAWAII
Director of Regulatory Agencies
Post Office Box 541
Honolulu, Hawaii 96809

IDAHO
Commissioner of Finance
Statehouse Annex 5
Boise, Idaho 83707

ILLINOIS
Commissioner of Banks and Trust Companies
Room 400
Reisch Building
4 West Old State Capitol Plaza
Springfield, Illinois 62701

INDIANA
Department of Financial Institutions
1024 Indiana State Office Building
Indianapolis, Indiana 46204

IOWA
Superintendent of Banking
607 Locust Street
Des Moines, Iowa 50309

KANSAS
State Bank Commissioner
Suite 600
818 Kansas Avenue
Topeka, Kansas 66612

KENTUCKY
Commissioner of Banking and Securities
Department of Banking
102 Mero Street
Frankfort, Kentucky 40601

LOUISIANA
Commissioner of Financial Institutions
Post Office Box 44095
Baton Rouge, Louisiana 70804

MAINE
Superintendent of Banks and Banking
Bureau of Banks and Banking
State Office Annex
Augusta, Maine 04330

MARYLAND
Bank Commissioner
2005 Blaustein Building
One North Charles Street
Baltimore, Maryland 21201

MASSACHUSETTS
Commissioner of Banks
State Office Building
100 Cambridge Street
Boston, Massachusetts 02202

MICHIGAN
Commissioner of Financial Institutions
Financial Institutions Bureau
Law Building
Lansing, Michigan 48913

MINNESOTA
Commissioner of Banks
Minnesota State Office Building
St. Paul, Minnesota 55155

MISSISSIPPI
State Comptroller
Department of Bank Supervision
Post Office Box 731
Jackson, Mississippi 39205

MISSOURI
Commissioner of Finance
Post Office Box 716
Jefferson City, Missouri 65101

MONTANA
Director
Department of Business Regulation
805 North Maine Street
Helena, Montana 59601

NEBRASKA
Director of Banking
1001 "O" Street
Lincoln, Nebraska 68508

NEVADA
Superintendent of Banks
Nye Building, Room 220
201 South Fall Street
Carson City, Nevada 89701

NEW HAMPSHIRE
Bank Commissioner
97 North Main Street
Concord, New Hampshire 03301

NEW JERSEY
Commissioner of Banking
State House Annex
Trenton, New Jersey 08625

NEW MEXICO
Commissioner of Banking
Lew Wallace Building
Santa Fe, New Mexico 87501

NEW YORK
Superintendent of Banks
11th Floor
100 Church Street
New York, New York 10007

NORTH CAROLINA
Commissioner of Banks
Post Office Box 951
Raleigh, North Carolina 27602

NORTH DAKOTA
Commissioner of Banking and Financial Institutions
1301 State Capitol
Bismarck, North Dakota 58501

OHIO
Superintendent of Banks
366 East Broad Street
Columbus, Ohio 43215

OKLAHOMA
Bank Commissioner
Suite 12
Lincoln Plaza
4545 North Lincoln
Oklahoma City, Oklahoma 73105

OREGON
Superintendent of Banks
Commerce Building
158 Twelfth Street, Northeast
Salem, Oregon 97310

PENNSYLVANIA
Secretary of Banking
Post Office Box 2155
Harrisburg, Pennsylvania 17120

PUERTO RICO
Secretary of the Treasury
Commonwealth of Puerto Rico
Post Office Box 4515
San Juan, Puerto Rico 00905

RHODE ISLAND
Bank Commissioner
169 Weybosset Street
Providence, Rhode Island 02903

SOUTH CAROLINA
Commissioner of Banking
State Board of Bank Control
1026 Sumter Street
Columbia, South Carolina 29201

SOUTH DAKOTA
Superintendent of Banks
Department of Banking and Finance
Pierre, South Dakota 57501

TENNESSEE
Superintendent of Banks
Capitol Hill Building, Suite 460
301 Seventh Avenue, North
Nashville, Tennessee 37219

TEXAS
Banking Commissioner
John H. Regan State Office Building
Austin, Texas 78701

UTAH
Commissioner of Financial Institutions
10 West Broadway
Salt Lake City, Utah 84101

VERMONT
Commissioner of Banking and Insurance
State Office Building
Montpelier, Vermont 05602

VIRGINIA
Commissioner of Banking
800 Blanton Building
Richmond, Virginia 23219

VIRGIN ISLANDS
Banking Board of the Virgin Islands
Charlotte Amalie
St. Thomas, Virgin Islands 00802

WASHINGTON
Supervisor of Banking
Room 111-B
General Administration Building
Olympia, Washington 98501

WEST VIRGINIA
Commissioner of Banking
Room B-406
State Office Building
1900 Washington Street, East
Charleston, West Virginia 25305

WISCONSIN
Commissioner of Banking
Room 401
30 West Mifflin Street
Madison, Wisconsin 53703

WYOMING
State Bank Examiner
Supreme Court Building
Cheyenne, Wyoming 82001

Your Federal Regulators

OFFICE OF THE ADMINISTRATOR OF NATIONAL BANKS
Comptroller of the Currency
United States Treasury
Washington, D.C. 20220

National Bank Regional Administrators:

Connecticut, Maine, Massachusetts, New Hampshire, Rhode Island, and Vermont

Suite P-400
Three Center Plaza
Boston, Massachusetts 02108

New York, New Jersey, Virgin Islands, and Puerto Rico
Room 520
33 Liberty Street
New York, New York 10005

Delaware and Pennsylvania
Suite 1316
Three Parkway
Philadelphia, Pennsylvania 19102

Indiana, Kentucky, and Ohio
One Erieview Plaza
Cleveland, Ohio 44114

Virginia, West Virginia, Washington, D.C., North Carolina, and Maryland
Room 5215
400 North Eighth Street
Richmond, Virginia 23240

Florida, Georgia, and South Carolina
1510 First National Bank Tower
2 Peachtree Street, Northwest
Atlanta, Georgia 30303

Illinois and Michigan
164 West Jackson Boulevard
Chicago, Illinois 60604

Mississippi, Alabama, Tennessee, Arkansas, and Louisiana
Room 1900
165 Madison Avenue
Memphis, Tennessee 38103

North Dakota, South Dakota, Wisconsin, and Minnesota
Room 300
822 Marquette Avenue
Minneapolis, Minnesota 55402

Iowa, Kansas, Missouri, and Nebraska
Suite 2616
911 Main Street
Kansas City, Missouri 64105

Texas and Oklahoma
Suite 4500
1401 Elm Street
Dallas, Texas 75202

Utah, Colorado, Arizona, Wyoming, and New Mexico
Suite 1800
1600 Broadway
Denver, Colorado 80202

Washington, Alaska, Idaho, Oregon, and Montana
Room 900
707 Southwest Washington Street
Portland, Oregon 97205

California, Hawaii, and Nevada
Suite 3939
555 California Street
San Francisco, California 94104

BOARD OF GOVERNORS OF THE FEDERAL RESERVE SYSTEM
Office of Saver and Consumer Affairs
or
Division of Banking Supervision and Regulation
Constitution Avenue
Washington, D.C. 20551

Federal Reserve District Banks:

Alabama, Florida, Georgia, and part of Louisiana, Mississippi, and Tennessee
Federal Reserve Bank of Atlanta
Federal Reserve Station
Atlanta, Georgia 30303

Maine, Massachusetts, New Hampshire, Rhode Island, and part of Connecticut
Federal Reserve Bank of Boston
30 Pearl Street
Boston, Massachusetts 02106

Iowa and part of Illinois, Indiana, Michigan, and Wisconsin
Federal Reserve Bank of Chicago
Box 834
Chicago, Illinois 60690

Ohio and part of Kentucky and Pennsylvania
Federal Reserve Bank of Cleveland
Post Office Box 6387
Cleveland, Ohio 44101

Texas and part of Arizona, Louisiana, New Mexico, and Oklahoma
Federal Reserve Bank of Dallas
Station K
Dallas, Texas 75222

Colorado, Kansas, Nebraska, Wyoming, and part of Missouri, New Mexico, and Oklahoma
Federal Reserve Bank of Kansas City
Federal Reserve Station
Kansas City, Missouri 64198

Minnesota, Montana, North Dakota, South Dakota, and part of Michigan and Wisconsin
Federal Reserve Bank of Minneapolis
Minneapolis, Minnesota 55440

New York and part of New Jersey and Connecticut
Federal Reserve Bank of New York
33 Liberty Street
New York, New York 10045

Delaware and part of New Jersey and Pennsylvania
Federal Reserve Bank of Philadelphia
925 Chestnut Street
Philadelphia, Pennsylvania 19101

Washington, D.C., Maryland, North Carolina, South Carolina, Virginia, and West Virginia
Federal Reserve Bank of Richmond
Post Office Box 27622
Richmond, Virginia 23261

Arkansas and part of Illinois, Indiana, Kentucky, Mississippi, Missouri, and Tennessee
Federal Reserve Bank of St. Louis
Post Office Box 442
St. Louis, Missouri 63166

Alaska, California, Hawaii, Idaho, Nevada, Oregon, Utah, Washington, and part of Arizona
Federal Reserve Bank of San Francisco
San Francisco, California 94120

FEDERAL DEPOSIT INSURANCE CORPORATION
550 Seventeenth Street, Northwest
Washington, D.C. 20429

FDIC Regional Directors:

Alabama, Florida, and Georgia
Suite 3030
2 Peachtree Street, Northwest
Atlanta, Georgia 30303

Connecticut, Maine, Massachusetts, New Hampshire, Rhode Island, and Vermont
Room 810
2 Center Plaza
Boston, Massachusetts 02108

Illinois and Indiana
Room 1500
164 West Jackson Boulevard
Chicago, Illinois 50504

Kentucky, Ohio, and West Virginia
Suite 600
37 West Broad Street
Columbus, Ohio 43215

Colorado, New Mexico, Oklahoma, and Texas
Suite 3300
300 North Ervay Street
Dallas, Texas 75201

Michigan and Wisconsin
Room 813
1 South Pinckney Street
Madison, Wisconsin 53703

Arkansas, Louisiana, Mississippi, and Tennessee
Suite 1010
165 Madison Avenue
Memphis, Tennessee 38103

Minnesota, Montana, North Dakota, South Dakota, and Wyoming
Suite 266
730 Second Avenue South
Minneapolis, Minnesota 55402

New Jersey, New York, Puerto Rico, and the Virgin Islands
21st Floor
345 Park Avenue
New York, New York 10022

Iowa and Nebraska
Suite 1200
1700 Farnam Street
Omaha, Nebraska 68102

Delaware, Maryland, and Pennsylvania
Suite 2901
5 Penn Center Plaza
Philadelphia, Pennsylvania 19103

Washington, D.C., North Carolina, South Carolina, and Virginia
Suite 435
908 East Main Street
Richmond, Virginia 23219

Kansas and Missouri
Suite 2909
720 Olive Street
St. Louis, Missouri 63101

Alaska, Arizona, California, Guam, Hawaii, Idaho, Nevada, Oregon, Utah, and Washington
Suite 3600
44 Montgomery Street
San Francisco, California 94104

FEDERAL HOME LOAN BANK BOARD
101 Indiana Avenue, Northwest
Washington, D.C. 20552

FHLB District Presidents:

Connecticut, Maine, Massachusetts, New Hampshire, Rhode Island, and Vermont
One Union Street
Boston, Massachusetts 02108

New Jersey, New York, Puerto Rico, and the Virgin Islands
Floor 103
One World Trade Center
New York, New York 10048

Delaware, Pennsylvania, and West Virginia
4th Floor
11 Stanwix Street
Gateway Center
Pittsburgh, Pennsylvania 15222

Alabama, Washington, D.C., Florida, Georgia, Maryland, North Carolina, South Carolina, and Virginia
Coastal States Building
260 Peachtree Street, Northwest
Atlanta, Georgia 30303

Kentucky, Ohio, and Tennessee
2500 DuBois Tower
Cincinnati, Ohio 45202

Indiana and Michigan
2900 Indiana Tower
One Indiana Square
Indianapolis, Indiana 46204

Illinois and Wisconsin
11 East Wacker Drive
Chicago, Illinois 60601

Iowa, Minnesota, Missouri, North Dakota, and South Dakota
Second Avenue at Center Street
Des Moines, Iowa 50309

Arkansas, Louisiana, Mississippi, New Mexico, and Texas
1400 Tower Building
Little Rock, Arkansas 72201

Colorado, Kansas, Nebraska, and Oklahoma
Seventh and Harrison Streets
Topeka, Kansas 66601

Arizona, Nevada, and California
Post Office Box 7948
600 California Street
San Francisco, California 94120

Alaska, Hawaii and Guam, Idaho, Montana, Oregon, Utah, Washington, and Wyoming
600 Stewart Street
Seattle, Washington 98101

NATIONAL CREDIT UNION ADMINISTRATION
2025 M Street, Northwest
Washington, D.C.

Connecticut, Maine, Massachusetts, New Hampshire, New York, Puerto Rico, Rhode Island, Virgin Islands, and Vermont
Room 3E
State Street South Building
1776 Heritage Drive
Boston, Massachusetts 02171

Washington, D.C., Delaware, Maryland, New Jersey, and Pennsylvania
Box 926
Federal Building
228 Walnut Street
Harrisburg, Pennsylvania 17108

Alabama, Canal Zone, Florida, Georgia, Kentucky, Mississippi, North Carolina, South Carolina, Tennessee, Virginia, and West Virginia
Room 500
800 Peachtree Street, Northeast
Atlanta, Georgia 30308

Illinois, Indiana, Iowa, Michigan, Minnesota, North Dakota, Ohio, South Dakota, and Wisconsin
Room 1003
New Federal Building
234 North Summit Street
Toledo, Ohio 43604

Arkansas, Colorado, Kansas, Louisiana, Missouri, Nebraska, New Mexico, Oklahoma, Texas, Utah, and Wyoming
Seventh Floor
205 West Ninth Street
Austin, Texas 78701

Alaska, California, Guam, Hawaii, Idaho, Montana, Nevada, Oregon, Washington, and Arizona
Room 809
760 Market Street
San Francisco, California 94102

Appendix 2

How to Calculate Interest

While the use of the Annual Percentage Rate (APR) makes it possible for potential borrowers to compare interest rates, they cannot easily determine the dollar amount of the interest they will have to pay. That was one advantage of the add-on rate, which was banned because it gave an artificially low interest-rate figure.

The consumer may want to transform the APR into the add-on rate for the purpose of determing the dollar cost of the loan. Most lenders will provide this information on request. If you wish to calculate the add-on rate, you can calculate it by this formula:

$$\text{add-on rate} = \frac{\text{APR} \times (\text{the number of months of loan} + 1)}{\text{twice the number of months of the loan}}$$

or

$$r = \frac{\text{APR}\ (n + 1)}{2n}$$

If you were to convert a one-year (12-month) loan at 13.47 APR into the add-on rate, the calculation would be:

$$r + \frac{13.47\ \ (12\ +\ 1)}{2\ (12)} = \frac{13.47\ (13)}{24} = 7.3 \text{ percent}$$

Be very careful. The formula allows for an error to enter the calculations that is significant for long-term loans. Use this calculation method only for loans of three years or less. It will provide a very close approximation of the actual charges.

The reason why it is difficult for the consumer to calculate the APR is that interest is levied each month (or sometimes each day) on the remaining balance of the principal. Thus, over the course of a loan, interest payments must be calculated many times. Of course, this is done in advance—at the time you borrow the money—but if you make payments either early or late, the actual amount of interest will differ from what you have been quoted.

The add-on method provided for determining the total amount of interest that would be paid and then tacking it onto the principal. Thus, to continue with our example, borrowing $1,000 at 7.3 percent would bring the total to $1,073, with monthly payments of $839.42. If you wished to prepay this loan, the amount of interest to be paid would be determined by the Rule of 78s. As indicated in Chapter 5, this can be more costly than prepayment under the APR system.

The mirror image of the add-on loan was the discount loan. Here the lender deducted the interest in advance. If a borrower wished to have $1,000 and the interest cost was $73, he or she would actually receive only $927. The borrower then paid back the full $1,000. The discount rate for this loan would actually be 7.9 percent, because the borrower would pay $73 for the use of $927.

Appendix 3
Surveys Used

Government

The Federal Reserve produces two surveys of banks of interest to the consumer. The monthly Federal Reserve *Bulletin* contains a table, "Finance Rates on Selected Types of Installment Credit," based on a survey of 350 banks. The Federal Reserve Bank of New York prepares annually the "Functional Cost Analysis," based on a survey of several hundred banks, which details the cost of the specific operations of banks.

The Federal Home Loan Bank Board conducts a survey to determine mortgage characteristics. The results arc published in the Fcderal Reserve *Bulletin* in the table "Terms and Yields on New Home Mortgages."

Industry Organizations

The American Bankers Association groups commercial banks. Every few years it conducts a survey of "Savings and Time Deposit Practices of Commercial Banks."

The National Association of Mutual Savings Banks includes those banks and publishes a *Directory,* which includes interest-rate data, and an annual *National Fact Book,* based on information received from all mutual savings banks.

The United States Savings and Loan League publishes an annual *Savings and Loan Fact Book,* which includes compilations of data from its own members and from government and other surveys.

The Credit Union National Association *Yearbook* contains

information on all credit unions, including average interest rates by state.

Consumer Surveys

In "Break the Banks! A Shopper's Guide to Banking Services," San Francisco Consumer Action includes data from a survey of sixteen major California banks.

The New York Consumer Assembly surveyed twenty-eight New York City and suburban banks in its May 1974 report on checking account costs.

The Maine Public Interest Research Group conducted a survey of banks in that state. As indicated in the Preface, data from this study were not used directly in this book.

Consumers Union surveyed eighty-seven banks in five cities in preparing its 1975 Guide to Banking Services. As in our own case, CU found that many banks refused to cooperate.

The Twentieth Century Fund conducted 300 interviews covering 70 banks in its study, *Conflicts of Interest: Commercial Bank Trust Departments.*

We surveyed about thirty banks and thrifts concerning their savings and time accounts, and another ten on their checking accounts. As with CU, we found that many banks will refuse to disclose information for a comparative study. Yet, if you actually go to each bank as a potential customer, this information is, of course, available.

Index